# A WORLD-CLASS
# EDUCATION

## ASCD MEMBER BOOK

Many ASCD members received this book as a
member benefit upon its initial release.

Learn more at: **www.ascd.org/memberbooks**

# VIVIEN STEWART

# A WORLD-CLASS
# EDUCATION

## LEARNING FROM INTERNATIONAL MODELS
## OF EXCELLENCE AND INNOVATION

**ASCD®**

LEARN. TEACH. LEAD.

Alexandria, Virginia USA

1703 N. Beauregard St. • Alexandria, VA 22311-1714 USA
Phone: 800-933-2723 or 703-578-9600 • Fax: 703-575-5400
Website: www.ascd.org • E-mail: member@ascd.org
Author guidelines: www.ascd.org/write

Gene R. Carter, *Executive Director;* Ed Milliken, *Chief Program Officer;* Carole Hayward, *Publisher;* Genny Ostertag, *Acquisitions Editor;* Julie Houtz, *Director, Book Editing & Production;* Katie Martin, *Editor;* Greer Wymond, *Senior Graphic Designer;* Mike Kalyan, *Production Manager;* Keith Demmons, *Desktop Publishing Specialist*

All web links in this book are correct as of the publication date but may have become inactive or otherwise modified since that time. If you notice a deactivated or changed link, please e-mail books@ascd.org with the words "Link Update" in the subject line. In your message, please specify the web link, the book title, and the page number on which the link appears.

ASCD Member Book, No. FY12-5 (Feb. 2012, P). ASCD Member Books mail to Premium (P), Select (S), and Institutional Plus (I+) members on this schedule: Jan., PSI+; Feb., P; Apr., PSI+; May, P; July, PSI+; Aug., P; Sept., PSI+; Nov., PSI+; Dec., P. Select membership was formerly known as Comprehensive membership.

PAPERBACK ISBN: 978-1-4166-1374-9          ASCD product #111016
Also available as an e-book (see Books in Print for the ISBNs).

Quantity discounts for the paperback edition only: 10–49 copies, 10%; 50+ copies, 15%; for 1,000 or more copies, call 800-933-2723, ext. 5634, or 703-575-5634. For desk copies: member@ascd.org.

**Library of Congress Cataloging-in-Publication Data**
Stewart, Vivien.
  A world-class education : learning from international models of excellence and innovation / Vivien Stewart.
    p. cm.
  Includes bibliographical references and index.
  ISBN 978-1-4166-1374-9 (pbk. : alk. paper)
  1. School improvement programs. 2. Education, Higher–Economic aspects. 3. Labor productivity—Effect of education on. 4. Education and globalization. I. Title.
  LB2822.82.S8418 2012
  371.2'07–dc23
                              2011041504

22 21 20 19 18 17 16 15 14 13 12          1 2 3 4 5 6 7 8 9 10 11 12

# A WORLD-CLASS EDUCATION

LEARNING FROM INTERNATIONAL MODELS
OF EXCELLENCE AND INNOVATION

# INTRODUCTION

Everything has changed, except the way we think. —**Albert Einstein**

The world is changing, and fast. The accelerating pace of globalization over the past 20 years—driven by profound technological changes, the rise of Asia (especially China and India), and the ever more rapid pace of scientific discovery—has produced a whole new way of life. Companies manufacture goods around the clock and around the world, ideas and events travel the Internet in seconds, a financial crisis in the United States affects the ability of farmers in Africa to borrow money for seed, and pollution in China affects the air in Los Angeles. The world in which today's students live is fundamentally different from the world in which we were raised. As never before, education in the United States must prepare students for a world where the opportunities for success require the ability to compete and cooperate on a global scale.

Technological, economic, and political trends have increased the demand for higher skills and reduced the demand for lower skills while intensifying the competition for quality jobs. Since 1990, more than 3 billion people in China, India, and the former Soviet Union have entered the global economy (Zakaria, 2008), and while these countries at first concentrated on creating low-skill jobs, they are increasingly aiming to become competitive and dynamic knowledge-based economies. In fact, countries around the world are trying to raise people out of poverty and respond to increasing popular pressure to provide more economic opportunities for the next generation through expanding education. No country wants to be just the shoe manufacturer of the world.

The global economy is not a zero-sum game in which only one country can be prosperous. An expanding middle class in other countries provides an expanding market for U.S. goods and services, and companies from newly expanding economies may build plants and create jobs in the United States. But the competition for high-skill and high-income jobs is indeed escalating, and the United States cannot maintain its standard of living unless it provides its citizens with a world-class education system.

It is therefore all the more alarming that in December 2010, when the 2009 results from the Organisation for Economic Co-operation and Development's (OECD's) Programme for International Student Assessment (PISA) were released, U.S. students once again scored well below those in other developed countries on tests of reading, math, and science. These mediocre results followed similar scores from the previous rounds of PISA in 2000, 2003, and 2006, as well as from the Trends in International Mathematics and Science Survey (TIMSS) conducted by the International Association for the Evaluation of Educational Achievement. In fact, the United States has a high proportion of students who do not even reach baseline levels of proficiency on PISA.

As educators, we care a lot about excellence and equity, but viewed through the lens of international comparisons, American K–12 education seems neither excellent nor equitable. But are these comparisons valid? Why should we pay attention to international assessments? We don't need an international assessment to tell us that many of our schools are not doing well; we have plenty of our own testing to tell us that. Are they just one more stick to bash teachers with? What can we learn from international comparisons that we can't learn from our own research and experiences?

When the media reports on international assessment results like a horse race, with winners and losers, these are understandable questions. However, they miss the point. In today's interconnected world, our students are not competing with students from the state or city next door, but with students from Singapore, Shanghai, and Stockholm. We owe it to our students to understand what is happening around the world. For their sake, we can't afford to give them an education that is lower in quality and less up-to-date than that which other countries are providing. Just as American businesses need to know what is happening in other countries if they hope be successful, we as educators need to understand global trends in education in order to create schools that equip our students for the world of tomorrow, not the world of yesterday.

Another reason for paying attention to international assessments is that, having now been implemented over a number of years, these assessments and their results have led to a growing body of research, observation, and discussion that goes beyond the numbers and rankings to help us understand why some systems are moving ahead rapidly and producing more equitable performance while others remain static and unequal. In the 20th century, the United States was the world leader in education. We were the first country to achieve universal secondary education and the first country to expand higher education beyond the elite class. However, in the 21st century, other countries are catching up and leaping ahead of us in high school graduation rates, in the quality and equity of performance in their K–12 education systems, and in the proportion of students graduating from college. Contrary to the beliefs of some pundits, American education has not gotten worse—but education in other parts of the world has gotten a lot better, a lot faster. How are countries that are outperforming our own K–12 education system doing it? What education policies and practices have they adopted? How do these differ from American educational practices? And are they relevant to the United States, or do they depend on a particular cultural context?

This book attempts to provide some answers to those questions by examining the following key issues:

• The major global trends that are transforming the skills needed and changing the shape of the global talent pool.

- How the U.S. education system compares with other education systems against the emerging world standards of excellence.
- How other countries have developed high-performing education systems and the lessons they hold for the United States.
- The common success factors that cut across these high-performing systems.
- Current international best practices in two key areas of education—*developing and maintaining a 21st century teaching and leadership profession* and *creating modern curriculum, instruction, and assessment systems.*
- How technology and international exchange can help the United States create a world-class educational system that is responsive to future challenges.

Let me stress at the outset of this book that there is no perfect education system. Globalization poses challenges for everyone. Every education system in the world struggles to some degree to keep up with the rapid pace of change. And countries face many similar challenges. For example, widespread internal and international migration have created more heterogeneous societies everywhere, placing new demands on educators as they respond to students and families from differing cultural and linguistic backgrounds. In addition to challenging schools to adapt to new populations, globalization also raises fundamental questions about whether the knowledge and skills needed by today's graduates will be significantly different from those that schools have provided in the past.

But other countries are demonstrating that large-scale educational acceleration is possible, even as our own educational performance has been flat for decades. Their success is not accidental, but the result of careful policy choice and effective implementation. Through combinations of national policies and leadership together with capacity building at the school level, these countries are achieving excellence in terms of student achievement, student retention, equity, and efficiency, and they are doing so at a lower cost than in the United States. Some may argue that the experiences of countries that are significantly smaller are not relevant to a country the size of the United States. But many of these countries are the size of American states and could therefore be looked at as models for state-based education systems. In addition, we can learn from countries that are significantly larger than ours and still making giant strides, such as India and China.

High-performing or rapidly improving countries are also intently focused on becoming learning systems, constantly updating their assessment of whether their education system is preparing their students for the rapidly changing global knowledge economy. As leaders contemplate changes in particular policies and practices, whether in science and math, teaching and leadership development, or early intervention, they routinely compare their countries' methods against research and best practices from all over the world, including the United States. This strategy, known as "international benchmarking," has become a critical tool for governments and educators as they seek to develop world-class education systems. Some are sending not just their policymakers and researchers to scour the world for international best practice, but also their principals and teachers; in the United States, we rarely do this.

This book has its roots in my own experience. After growing up and being educated in England, I traveled to Africa, where I studied the relationships among education, economic development, and nation building. I then moved to the United States, where I worked for a number of years at Carnegie Corporation, directing its children, youth, and education programs. I was engaged in many efforts to improve American education, including implementing early childhood education, reforming urban schools, promoting healthy adolescent development, and improving the teaching profession. In the 1990s, my work with Carnegie Corporation also allowed me to see firsthand the changes in schools and universities in the former Soviet Union and Eastern Europe after the end of the Cold War. Later, in a stint as a senior education advisor at the United Nations, I worked on providing education to refugees around the world and restarting schools for children affected by war. Finally, in my eight years as the vice president for education of Asia Society, I witnessed the extraordinary rise of Asia, traveling extensively on that continent and conferring with many educators and political and business leaders about the growth and challenges of Asian economies and education systems.

The privilege of being exposed to all these international experiences brought home to me just how dramatic the current global transformations are—comparable in scale and scope to the Industrial Revolution. The thirst for knowledge is universal, and education's importance to societies is now almost universally appreciated. Getting education right gives a country a powerful platform on which to build a healthy economy and a healthy society. Getting it wrong can hold back a country for years to come, especially in this new borderless knowledge economy, where human capital is the greatest asset most countries have.

As I have engaged in education efforts over the course of my career, I have tried to understand why, in the post–Cold War era, many countries have leaped ahead while the United States, once a world leader in education, has barely improved its performance over the past 20 years. What are the ingredients not just of *effective schools* but of *effective systems?* This book combines my own firsthand experience and observations of education systems in different parts of the globe with the small but growing research literature on these questions. My fundamental concerns are that the United States is being harmed economically and socially, as well as in terms of its ability to deal with the rest of the world, by its slow educational response to globalization, and that until very recently, our country has largely ignored the vigorous global conversation about educational performance and innovation.

There are many important initiatives underway to improve education in the United States on a wide range of fronts. We have many wonderful schools and "pockets of excellence," and our research and educational innovation are second to none. But this is not a book about those efforts, important as they are. Rather, its aim is to make educators aware of the new global context and standards of excellence by examining the experiences of countries that have surpassed or will soon surpass the United States educationally for the purpose of understanding what U.S. schools might do differently and better.

Chapter 1 examines the great transformation that is taking place around the world and the need for the United States to become more internationally competitive. Chapter 2 describes the immense educational improvements made in recent years in Singapore, Canada, Finland, China, and Australia, and analyzes some key lessons. Education and political leaders in these countries did not pursue identical policies, but Chapter 3 draws out common themes and elements and suggests areas for reflection for those looking to improve education in the United States. Chapter 4 examines international lessons in building a high-quality teaching and school leadership profession. Chapter 5 proposes how curriculum, instruction, and assessment need to be modernized to give our students the knowledge and skills to prepare for the 21st century. Finally, Chapter 6 looks at what kind of efforts will be needed to create a world-class education system that will carry the United States into the future.

My visits to schools around the world have led me to ponder the key ingredients of successful school systems. Is it money? Is it culture? How do communities and countries move from having poor or highly unequal schools to good or even great schools? What are the political and economic contexts that drive reform? What education policies did governments pursue or not pursue? How did they assure quality? Equal opportunity? How did they ensure good teachers? My goal in writing this book is to add to the conversation about developing world-class schools in the United States and to engage more educators in considering the possibilities in international experience. What high-performing countries show is that performance does not have to be flat, that substantial improvement on a wide scale is possible, and that both excellence and equity are attainable. By looking at the lessons to be learned from countries that have effectively ramped up their educational performance and considering how they might be adapted in our national context, we can broaden the range of options under consideration and draw on a wider evidence base. Because international benchmarking in education is relatively new and the experiences of many countries and many educational issues have not yet been thoroughly researched, no book can yet be definitive about what can be learned from education systems around the world. However, just as a businessperson today cannot afford *not* to benchmark his or her industry against the best in the world, we as educators cannot afford to isolate ourselves educationally. The yardstick for judging educational success is no longer national but international, and international benchmarking can be an important tool for improvement.

Learning goes both ways. Other countries have learned a great deal from the United States in the past, and I believe it is time for American educators to adopt a new worldview, to be open to others' practice, and to be willing to share our own experience. This is an enormously resourceful country with great assets. If we now engage with the world's knowledge about globalization and education, and if we build on and modernize our own assets more effectively, we can indeed have a world-class education system for our children and grandchildren.

# 1

# GLOBALIZATION AND EDUCATION

If Americans are to continue to prosper and to exercise leadership in this new global context, it is imperative that we understand the new global forces that we have both shaped and had thrust upon us. The alternative is to be at their mercy. **—Edward Fiske**

## The World Transformed

We used to think that people who thought the Earth was flat were uneducated. But Thomas Friedman's best-selling book, *The World Is Flat* (2005), helped us to understand that if the world is not exactly flat, then it is deeply interconnected as never before. Friedman's book described how technology and the fall of trade barriers have led to the integration of markets and nations, and enabled individuals, companies, and nation-states to reach around the world faster and cheaper than ever before. We see evidence of this interconnectedness in our lives every day—from the food we eat to the coffee we drink to the clothes we wear. Sports teams recruit talent from around the globe, and the iPhones we use to communicate are manufactured in more than 19 different countries.

This transformation of the world has happened relatively recently and in a short period of time. The economic liberalization of China beginning in the 1980s, the development of democracy in South Korea in 1987, and the fall of the Soviet Union and the development of free trade treaties in the early 1990s introduced 3 billion people, previously locked into their own national economies, into the global economy. Harvard economist Richard Freeman calls this the "great doubling" of the global labor force (National Governors Association, Council of Chief State School Officers, and Achieve, Inc., 2008, p. 9). In the late 1990s, the wiring of the world in preparation for the "millennium bug" unleashed another set of sweeping changes, as did the 2001 accession of China to the World Trade Organization and the 2003 economic liberalization of India, which jump-started that country's tremendous growth. The results have been staggering. Twenty years ago, bicycles were China's primary method of transportation, the G7 group represented the most powerful nations on earth, and the World Wide Web was just a proposal (McKinsey, 2011). Who at that time would have imagined the dramatic skyline of Shanghai today, that the G7 would become the G20, and that mobile web use would be growing exponentially around the world?

The effects of globalization have been far-reaching. While the living standards of the world are still highly uneven, 400 million people have moved out of extreme poverty since 1980—more than at any other time in human history. The growth and urbanization of a global middle class is creating huge new markets for goods and services of all kinds. Since 2000, despite frequent political and economic crises that cause it to dip temporarily, the global economy has been expanding (Zakaria, 2008). The world's economic center of gravity is also shifting: 50 percent of growth in gross domestic product (GDP) occurs outside the developed world, a fact that is fundamentally changing business models. Already, one in five U.S. jobs is tied to exports, and that proportion will increase (U.S. Census Bureau, 2004).

Globalization is often viewed as a zero-sum game in which one nation's economic growth comes at the expense of another. But the reality is more complicated than that. While manufacturing has largely moved out of the developed world into countries with lower labor costs, the exponential growth of the economies of India and China and the smaller-scale growth of other economies such as Russia and Brazil, have also created enormous demand for U.S. products—high-end industrial goods, cars, luxury items, agricultural products, and so on—and have increased the numbers of tourists coming to the United States and the numbers of undergraduate and graduate students flocking to American universities. Large multinational companies from other countries are building plants and providing jobs in the United States, and the lower prices of consumer goods from abroad benefit the American consumer. Still, while the global integration of economies has created complex webs of capital, trade, information, currencies, services, supply chains, capital markets, information technology grids, and technology platforms that form a more intricate, multifaceted system than a model of simple economic competition among nations, the competition for industries and for high-skill, high-wage jobs has undoubtedly become more intense.

This intensified competition stems from several sources. First, automation has eliminated large numbers of lower-skill jobs—far more than outsourcing has, in fact. Second, the "death of distance" caused by the global spread of technology, which makes it just as easy to create a work team around the world as it is to create one across a company, has put American workers in direct competition with workers elsewhere. Work that can be digitized can now be done with the click of a mouse by anyone from virtually anywhere in the world. Jobs in medical diagnostics, architectural drawing, filmmaking, tax preparation, and call centers are some of the types of occupations that have been outsourced. American students today are therefore competing not just with students in the city or state next door but with students in Singapore and Shanghai, Bangalore and Helsinki.

As the economy has become not just more global but also more knowledge based, the skill mix in the economy has changed dramatically. The proportion of workers in blue-collar and administrative support positions in the United States dropped from 56 percent to 39 percent between 1969 and 1999, leaving a trail of rust-belt neighborhoods and cities. Meanwhile, the proportion of jobs that are managerial, professional, and technical increased from 23 percent to 33 percent during the same period (Levy & Murnane, 2004). Skill demands within jobs are increasing too. Jobs that require routine manual or cognitive tasks are rapidly being taken over by computers or lower-paid workers in other countries, while jobs that require higher levels of education and more sophisticated problem-solving and communication skills are in increasingly high demand. The jobs that once supported a middle-class standard of living for workers with a high school diploma or less have substantially disappeared. These new economic realities and rapid shifts in the job market are fundamentally changing what we need from our education system.

The rapid increase in emerging markets also means economic growth and the need to prepare students for jobs that require new skill sets. According to the Committee for Economic Development (2006) "to compete successfully in a global marketplace, both U.S.-based multinationals as well as small businesses, increasingly need employees with knowledge of foreign languages and cultures to market products to customers around the globe and to work effectively with foreign employees and partners in other countries" (pp. 1–2).

And it is not just the economy that has become more global. The most pressing issues of our time know no boundaries. Challenges facing the United States—from environmental degradation and global warming, to terrorism and weapons proliferation, to energy and water shortages, to pandemic diseases—spill across borders. The only way to address these challenges successfully will be through international cooperation among governments and organizations of all kinds. As the line between domestic and international continues to blur, American citizens will increasingly be called upon to vote and act on issues that require greater understanding of other cultures and greater knowledge of the 95 percent of the world outside our borders.

In the 20th century the United States was "the most powerful nation since Imperial Rome" (Zakaria, 2008, p. 217), dominating the world economically, culturally, politically, and militarily. While the United States still remains a military superpower and supports the world's largest economy, the rapid economic growth and expansion happening in other countries show that a country's global position cannot be taken for granted. A great transformation is taking place around the world—and it is taking place in education, as well.

## The Growing Global Talent Pool

In the second half of the 20th century, the United States was indeed the global leader in education. It was the first country to achieve mass secondary education. And while European countries stuck to their elite higher education systems, the United States dramatically expanded higher education opportunities through measures like the G.I. Bill after World War II. As a result, the United States has had the largest supply of highly qualified people in its adult labor force of any country in the world. This tremendous stock of highly educated human capital helped the United States to become the dominant economy in the world and to take advantage of the globalization and expansion of markets.

However, over the last two decades, countries around the globe have been focused on expanding education as the key to maximizing individual well-being, reducing poverty, and increasing economic growth. Under the Education for All initiative, one of the United Nations' Millennium Development Goals, nations have joined together with the goal of providing universal primary education in every country, especially the poorest countries, by 2015. Although there is still a long way to go to meet this goal, particularly in sub-Saharan Africa, among girls, and in war-torn areas, more than 33 million children were added to school rolls between 2000 and 2008 (UNESCO, 2010). Countries in the middle tier of economic development aspire to universal secondary school graduation. And the most developed countries have set the goal of greatly increased levels of college attendance.

Because of dramatic global educational gains, high school graduation has now become the norm in most industrialized countries. The Organisation for Economic Co-operation and Development (OECD) reports that by 2009, the United States had fallen from 1st in the world to 8th in the proportion of young adults (ages 18 to 24) receiving a high school diploma within the calendar year. This lower position does not indicate a drop in U.S. graduation levels; rather, it testifies to the success other nations have had ambitiously expanding their secondary school systems and raising their graduation rates. Although the United States actually showed a modest increase in secondary school graduation from 1995 to 2009, this achievement is dwarfed by the striking gains of a number of countries (see Figure 1). Among the 28 OECD countries with comparable data for 2009, the United States ranked 12th in the percent of the overall population (including adults over the age of 24) achieving secondary school graduation, which is 15 or more percentage points behind countries such as Portugal, Slovenia, Finland, Japan, Ireland, and Norway (OECD, 2011).

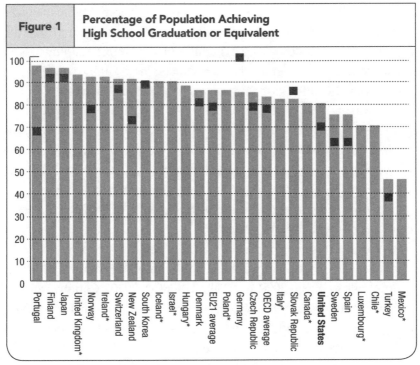

| Figure 1 | **Percentage of Population Achieving High School Graduation or Equivalent** |

■ 2009  ■ 1995   *Note:* *1995 figures not available. EU21 = Average of countries in the European Union.

*Source:* Data from Table A2.1 (Upper secondary graduation rates [2009] and Table A2.2 (Trends in graduate rates at upper secondary level [1995–2009]. OECD. (2011). *Education at a Glance 2011: OECD Indicators.* Paris: OECD Publishing.

The pace of change in high school graduation in some countries has been astounding. For example, two generations ago, South Korea had a similar economic output to Mexico and ranked 24th in education among the current 30 OECD countries. Today, South Korea is in the top 10 countries in terms of high school graduation rates, significantly ahead of the United States (Uh, 2008).

At the higher education level, the United States has a strong system that is admired around the world and is a world leader in research. According to the 2010 Times Higher Education World University rankings, 18 of the top 20 universities in the world were in America. And the United States is among the world leaders in the proportion of 35- to 64-year-olds with college degrees, reflecting the enormous expansion resulting from the G.I. Bill and, subsequently, the large numbers of people in the baby boom generation who went to college. But the United States falls to 10th place in the rankings when it comes to the proportion of younger adults age 25 to 34 who have an associate's degree or higher (National Center for Public Policy and Higher Education, 2008).

As recently as 1995, the United States tied for first in university and college graduation rates. But by 2008, it ranked 15th among 29 countries with comparable data, behind countries such as Australia, New Zealand, Japan, United Kingdom, Switzerland, and France. In the 1990s, when the importance of a highly educated workforce in the global economy was becoming ever clearer, other countries began to dramatically expand their higher education systems, as the United States had done in earlier decades. But during that period, there was almost no increase in the college-going rate in the United States. In addition, U.S. college dropout rates are high: only 54 percent of those who enter American colleges and universities complete a degree, compared with the OECD average of 71 percent. In Japan, the completion rate is 91 percent (National Center for Public Policy and Higher Education, 2008). Overall, the United States has lost ground in such international comparisons as the pace of higher education expansion has accelerated around the globe. While *older* generations of Americans are better educated than their international peers, many other countries have a higher proportion of *younger* workers with completed college degrees (National Center for Public Policy and Higher Education, 2008; see Figure 2).

This development of educated talent around the globe means that, going forward, the United States will not have the most educated workforce in the world as it has had in the past. Nowhere is this expansion of education more dramatic than in Asia.

## The Challenge from Asia

The rise of Asia is one of the most critical developments of the late 20th and early 21st centuries. From 1980 to 1990, Japan boomed, with

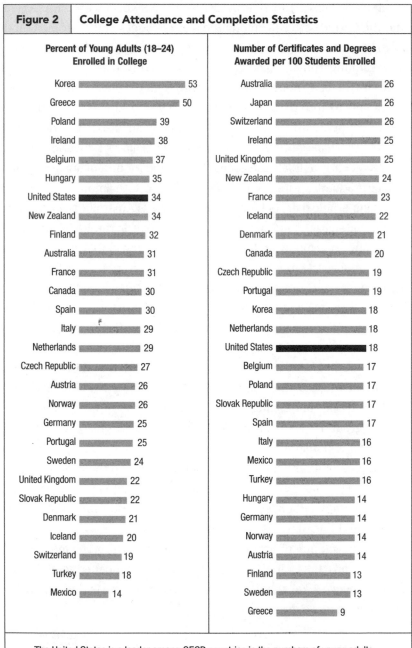

| Figure 2 | College Attendance and Completion Statistics |

**Percent of Young Adults (18–24) Enrolled in College**

|  | |
|---|---|
| Korea | 53 |
| Greece | 50 |
| Poland | 39 |
| Ireland | 38 |
| Belgium | 37 |
| Hungary | 35 |
| United States | 34 |
| New Zealand | 34 |
| Finland | 32 |
| Australia | 31 |
| France | 31 |
| Canada | 30 |
| Spain | 30 |
| Italy | 29 |
| Netherlands | 29 |
| Czech Republic | 27 |
| Austria | 26 |
| Norway | 26 |
| Germany | 25 |
| Portugal | 25 |
| Sweden | 24 |
| United Kingdom | 22 |
| Slovak Republic | 22 |
| Denmark | 21 |
| Iceland | 20 |
| Switzerland | 19 |
| Turkey | 18 |
| Mexico | 14 |

**Number of Certificates and Degrees Awarded per 100 Students Enrolled**

|  | |
|---|---|
| Australia | 26 |
| Japan | 26 |
| Switzerland | 26 |
| Ireland | 25 |
| United Kingdom | 25 |
| New Zealand | 24 |
| France | 23 |
| Iceland | 22 |
| Denmark | 21 |
| Canada | 20 |
| Czech Republic | 19 |
| Portugal | 19 |
| Korea | 18 |
| Netherlands | 18 |
| United States | 18 |
| Belgium | 17 |
| Poland | 17 |
| Slovak Republic | 17 |
| Spain | 17 |
| Italy | 16 |
| Mexico | 16 |
| Turkey | 16 |
| Hungary | 14 |
| Germany | 14 |
| Norway | 14 |
| Austria | 14 |
| Finland | 13 |
| Sweden | 13 |
| Greece | 9 |

The United States is a leader among OECD countries in the numbers of young adults enrolled in college, but ranks in the bottom half with regard to college completion.

*Source:* From *Measuring Up 2008: The National Report Card on Higher Education* (p. 8), by the National Center for Public Policy and Higher Education, 2008, San Jose, CA: Author. Available: http://measuringup2008.highereducation. org/print/NCPPHEMUNationalRpt.pdf world-class companies like Sony, Honda, Toyota, and Nissan achieving great success in industries where the United States had once been dominant. The so-called "Asian tigers"—South Korea, Singapore, and Hong Kong—leapt forward and developed influential economies out of all proportion to their tiny size. China's GDP tripled between 1980 and 2003, increasing from USD$12 trillion to USD$36 trillion, making it the world's second-largest economy; it is expected to grow to USD$60 trillion by 2020 (Tierney, 2006). If current economic growth rates continue, it's only a matter of time before China overtakes the United States as the world's largest economy. Since India liberalized its economic policies in 2003, its economy, like China's, has been growing at a rate of 8 to 9 percent per year; by 2030, India is expected to overtake China as the nation with the largest population in the world, leading it to become a potentially even more significant player in the global market.

During this period, hundreds of millions of people have risen from poverty to form an enormous new middle class. But while Asia's extraordinary economic growth is the stuff of daily business headlines, less well-known is the region's equally remarkable educational trajectory. Of the 65 countries and provinces participating in OECD's 2009 Programme for International Student Assessment (PISA), the results of which were released in December 2010, most of the top performers were in Asia. Shanghai and Hong Kong led the way, followed by Singapore, South Korea, and Japan.

In terms of scale, the challenge to the United States has only just begun. A fundamental shift in the global talent pool is under way. Looking ahead to 2020, the U.S. proportion of that global talent pool will shrink even further as China and India, with their enormous populations, rapidly expand their secondary and higher education systems (see Figure 3). In the Cultural Revolution of the 1960s in China, there were almost no students in school. Today, nine years of basic education are universal in all but the most remote areas, and China's goal is to have 90 percent of students in upper secondary school by 2020. If the U.S. high school graduation rate remains flat and China continues on its current path, China will be graduating a higher proportion of students from high school within a decade. And China has 200 million students in elementary and secondary education, compared with our about 66 million.

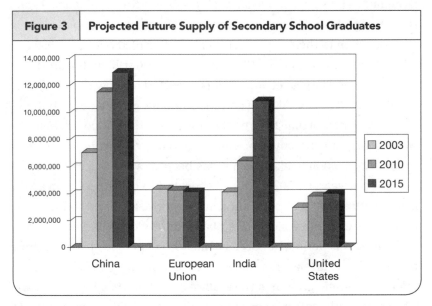

| Figure 3 | Projected Future Supply of Secondary School Graduates |

*Source:* From "Seeing U.S. Education Through the Prism of International Comparison" (slide 13). Presentation by A. Schleicher at a meeting of the Alliance for Excellence in Education, Washington, DC, October 4, 2007. Adapted with permission.

At the college level, according to the Chinese Ministry of Education, China has more than 82 million people who have received higher education, a small proportion of the population but still a number greater than America's 31 million college graduates. China expanded the number of students in higher education from 6 million in 1998 to 31 million in 2010, going from almost 10 percent to about 24 percent of the age cohort (Chinese Ministry of Education, 2010; see Figure 4). And many of these students are studying science and engineering. Harold Varmus, Nobel laureate, head of the National Cancer Institute, and cochair of the President's Council of Advisors on Science and Technology, observed, "In the 20th century, U.K. observers saw U.S. education as overtaking the United Kingdom. In the 21st century, arguably, China may soon be exceeding the United States in education" (Varmus, 2009).

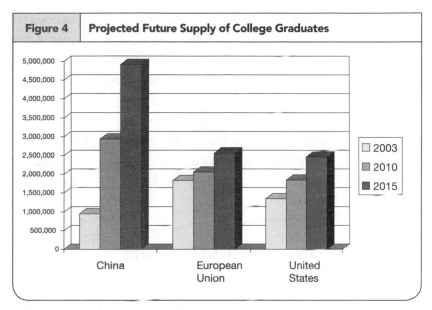

| Figure 4 | Projected Future Supply of College Graduates |

*Source:* From "Seeing U.S. Education Through the Prism of International Comparison" (slide 14). Presentation by A. Schleicher at a meeting of the Alliance for Excellence in Education, Washington, DC. October 1, 2007. Adapted with permission.

India has been behind other countries in expanding secondary education; currently, only 40 percent of students of an age to be enrolled in secondary school actually are. But having succeeded in massively expanding primary education over the past two decades, India is now making major investments in secondary education, with the goal of universalizing lower secondary education by 2017 and sharply increasing enrollments in upper secondary school. The Indian government established a National Knowledge Commission (2006–2009) to make recommendations for policies that would help establish a "vibrant, knowledge-based society" based on research, technology transfer, and knowledge and skill development and, thus, strengthen India's competitive position in the global knowledge economy (National Knowledge Commission, 2009). According to Montek Singh, deputy chairman of the Indian Planning Commission, "India is on the threshold of launching a new secondary education program, where we will deliberate, among other things, on how to achieve world class standards in science, math, and technology and how to build an education environment that fosters innovation" (Asia Society, 2008b, p. 6). At the higher education level, less than 10 percent of the age group is enrolled in postsecondary education, and many college courses are considered of low quality and relevance. However, India's elite Indian Institutes of Technology, modeled on the Massachusetts Institute of Technology and other premier scientific and technical institutions around the world, have produced graduates who have created software development and research and development companies from India to Silicon Valley, and who have catapulted into leading posts in global firms.

## The United States Fails World Standards of Excellence and Equity

Not only is the United States falling behind in terms of education *quantity,* but there is also increasing alarm about the *quality* of its education. A range of international assessments reveal disturbing weaknesses in American K–12 students' performance compared to that of their peers in other countries.

Three different international testing programs measure student performance in reading, math, and science on a regular basis. Trends in International Mathematics and Science Survey (TIMSS), a test of science knowledge in 4th, 8th, and 12th grades, and the Progress in International Reading Literacy Study (PIRLS), a test of 4th grade literacy, are produced by the International Association for the Evaluation of Educational Achievement (IEA). The Programme for International Student Assessment (PISA), produced by OECD and administered every 3 years, measures performance in math, science, and reading for 15-year-olds. These tests are administered to a randomly selected sample of students within the countries they assess so that their results can be generalized to the larger population. After successive administrations, the results of these tests provide a picture of how countries are changing over time in various areas.

## TIMSS

Beginning in 1995, with the most recent cycle of assessments taking place in 2007, TIMSS uses multiple-choice questions to assess learning of the science and math content commonly found in most countries' school curricula in particular grades. (A list of countries participating in TIMSS can be found online at http://nces.ed.gov/timss/countries. asp.). Students in the United States perform better on TIMSS than on PISA (see below), coming in 9th place in 8th grade math and 11th place in 8th grade science in 2007 (Quek et al., 2008), in part because not all of the higher-performing industrialized countries participate in TIMSS, and also because American students are used to multiple-choice tests that ask them to reproduce curriculum content. However, when the United States' TIMSS performance was compared with that of only the most developed nations in 2003, it ranked below the average of the 12 countries (Ginsburg, Leinwand, Anstrom, & Pollock, 2005).

## PIRLS

The second cycle of PIRLS took place in 2006 in 40 countries (participants can be found at http://pirls.bc.edu/pirls2006/countries.html). PIRLS measures 4th grade reading and tries to determine how policies and practices in and out of schools relate to reading engagement and achievement. The United States tends to do better on international assessments of reading than of math and science. In fact, it ranked 18th out of 40 countries, above the average performance. However, whereas other countries showed significant improvement between the two cycles of PIRLS, U.S. performance remained flat.

## PISA

The most widely used global student measures are the PISA assessments from OECD, which began in 2000 measuring performance in 43 countries and subsequently grew to include 60 countries and 5 nonnational systems in its 2009 surveys. Together, these countries constitute 90 percent of the global economy. In 2009, a number of provinces in mainland China took part in the PISA surveys for the first time, and

India is planning to participate in future surveys. PISA truly has become a global education report card.

The PISA assessments, given to 15-year-olds, differ from TIMSS in that their goal is not primarily to measure subject matter knowledge but to determine how well students near the end of compulsory schooling apply their knowledge to real-life situations. The emphasis is therefore on understanding of concepts, mastery of processes, and real-world problem solving. PISA reports the average score for students in each country and identifies the top performers (levels 5 and 6) and poor performers (levels 1 and 2). The most recent United States performance on PISA (OECD, 2010b) is disappointing, to say the least, in all three subject areas (see Figure 5).

**Science.** In science, U.S. students ranked 17th among OECD member countries in 2009 (23rd among all nations and provinces taking the test). The U.S. score of 502 is average among OECD members. However, 18 percent of U.S. students did not reach level 2, considered the baseline level for being able to use science and technology in everyday life. This was an improvement from 24.4 percent in 2006. At the top end of performance, the United States has roughly the same proportion of high scorers as in 2006, with 10 percent of students reaching levels 5 and 6. Compare this figure with 28 percent in Shanghai, China, and 22 percent in Finland.

**Math.** In math, the United States ranks 25th among OECD member countries (31st among all nations and entities taking the test). The U.S. score of 487 is below the average for OECD member countries, with 23.4 percent of students not reaching baseline level 2. Only 12 percent of American students reach level 5 or 6, compared with 50 percent in Shanghai, China, and over 30 percent in Singapore and Hong Kong, China.

**Reading.** In reading, the United States ranks 14th among OECD member countries. The U.S. score of 500 is average for OECD countries and is unchanged since 2000. Eighteen percent of American students do not reach baseline level 2 in reading and are therefore unlikely to be able to cope with postsecondary education or training. However, with 11.5 percent of students reaching levels 5 and 6, the United States has an above-average share of the highest performers—though it still ranks below Australia, Canada, and Singapore (OECD, 2011b).

| Figure 5 | Average Scores for Countries Ranking Above the United States in Reading, Mathematics, and Science on the 2009 PISA | | | | |
|----------|----------|-------|----------|-------|----------|-------|
| Reading | | | Mathematics | | Science | |
| Country/Region | Score | Country/Region | Score | Country/Region | Score |
| Shanghai, China | 556 | Shanghai, China | 600 | Shanghai, China | 575 |
| Korea | 539 | Singapore | 562 | Finland | 554 |
| Finland | 536 | Hong Kong, China | 555 | Hong Kong, China | 549 |
| Hong Kong, China | 533 | Korea | 546 | Singapore | 542 |
| Singapore | 526 | Chinese Taipei | 543 | Japan | 539 |
| Canada | 524 | Finland | 541 | Korea | 538 |
| New Zealand | 521 | Liechtenstein | 536 | New Zealand | 532 |
| Japan | 520 | Switzerland | 534 | Canada | 529 |
| Australia | 515 | Japan | 529 | Estonia | 528 |
| Netherlands | 508 | Canada | 527 | Australia | 527 |
| Belgium | 506 | Netherlands | 526 | Netherlands | 522 |
| Norway | 503 | Macao, China | 525 | Chinese Taipei | 520 |
| Estonia | 501 | New Zealand | 519 | Germany | 520 |
| Switzerland | 501 | Belgium | 515 | Liechtenstein | 520 |
| Poland | 500 | Australia | 514 | Switzerland | 517 |
| Iceland | 500 | Germany | 513 | United Kingdom | 514 |
| United States | 500 | Estonia | 512 | Slovenia | 512 |
| | | Iceland | 507 | Macao, China | 511 |
| | | Denmark | 503 | Poland | 508 |
| | | Slovenia | 501 | Ireland | 508 |
| | | Norway | 498 | Belgium | 507 |
| | | France | 497 | Hungary | 503 |
| | | Slovak Republic | 497 | United States | 502 |
| | | Austria | 496 | | |
| | | Poland | 495 | | |
| | | Sweden | 494 | | |
| | | Czech Republic | 493 | | |
| | | United Kingdom | 492 | | |
| | | Hungary | 490 | | |
| | | Luxembourg | 489 | | |
| | | United States | 487 | | |

*Source:* Comparing countries' performance in reading, mathematics, and science (Figures 2.16, 2.17, and 2.18). OECD (2011b), *Lessons from PISA for the United States: Strong Performers and Successful Reformers in Education.* Paris: OECD Publishing. http://dx.doi.org/10.1787/9789264096660-en. Used with permission.

The United States is not among the top performers in any of the three subjects tested by PISA. Despite some improvements in science, U.S. performance is average at best and largely flat. While small differences in scores on the PISA scale matter little, the performance gap between the United States and top-performing nations is huge. American students lag a full year behind their peers in the countries that score highest in math. Factoring into the U.S. performance are large variations in scores by region and by socioeconomic status. In other nations, large enough samples of students take the test to enable comparisons among states or provinces. The United States' sample size is not commensurately large, but the sample does enable approximate regional estimates that show that states in the Northeast and Midwest do better than states in the West or South. U.S. average performance is also strongly affected by the high proportion of students achieving scores at the bottom two levels. This continuing class- and race-based achievement gap means that we are failing to prepare large numbers of our young people, especially those in our minority communities, for postsecondary education or training. But we also lack a high proportion of students who reach the top skill levels that are critical for innovation and economic growth. Even our best and brightest are not achieving the way they should be.

In sum, the results from the world's global education report cards show that American students are not well prepared to compete in today's knowledge economy. A host of developed nations are surpassing us in education. These results are especially disturbing in light of the fact that the United States reports the world's second-highest per-pupil expenditure.

## What Can We Learn from International Comparisons?

How valid are these international assessments? Can we really use them to compare U.S. educational performance with that in other countries? Those who challenge the validity of using international assessments to compare educational systems do so based on a number of assumptions, all of which have largely turned out to be wrong:

1. *Other countries test a more select group of students than the United States does.* This was true for the early TIMSS assessments in the 1980s but is not, by and large, true today. According to Jim Hull, who examined international assessments for the National School Boards Association, "Since the 1990s, due to better sampling techniques and a move by more countries to universal education, the results represent the performance of the whole student population, including students who attend public, private, and vocational schools; students with special needs; and students who are not native speakers of their nation's language" (NGA et al., 2008, p. 20).

2. *Other countries are less diverse than the United States.* The United States is a diverse country, but so are most industrialized countries these days due to greatly increased international migration. While some countries that outperform the United States are culturally homogeneous, like Finland, many are not. In 2006, of the 11 other OECD countries that, like the United States, had a student population that was 10 percent immigrant, all performed higher that the United States in math and 9 performed higher in science. In addition, a lack of diversity is not a guarantee of educational success. Finland used to have relatively low-quality schools despite its cultural homogeneity. Its high performance today can be traced to education policies put in place over the past 20 years.

3. *The assessments favor test-oriented cultures like those in Asia.* The highest-performing countries or regions—Finland, Canada, Japan, Shanghai, Hong Kong, Singapore, Australia, and New Zealand—exist on four continents with different cultural backgrounds.

4. *Wealthier countries spend more on education than the United States does.* The United States is wealthier and spends more on education than most other countries. Among the 30 OECD countries, the United States has the highest GDP per capita and the second-highest educational expenditures. Only Luxembourg spends more per student.

5. *The United States' poor performance is due to high levels of poverty, not low levels of school quality.* In every country, students from higher-income backgrounds achieve at higher levels than lower-income

students. As the United States has a highly unequal income distribution, this is certainly a factor in U.S. performance. However, even America's most affluent students do not do as well as affluent students in other industrialized nations. Also, while the United States does not have a higher proportion of disadvantaged students than many other countries, the socioeconomic differences translate more strongly into student performance. In other words, the educational policies and practices of other countries do a more effective job of supporting lower-income students and equalizing educational opportunities.

There are clear limitations to these international assessments. One is that they only regularly measure three subject areas. It is possible that if other areas were measured, American students would perform better than students from other countries. For example, an IEA study of citizenship education found that American students perform relatively well compared with their international peers in their understanding of democratic institutions, an important goal of schooling (Torney-Purta, Lehmann, Oswald, & Schulz, 2001). However, they performed far less well in knowledge of other countries, an increasingly important need in the 21st century. And although there are no international assessments of proficiency in non-native languages, examining other countries' policies shows that most industrialized countries require study of a second language starting in elementary school and continuing for several years, whereas fewer than half of all American high school students take even one year of a foreign language, usually at the introductory level (American Council on the Teaching of Foreign Languages, 2010). What this means is that many of the students in high-performing countries who do well in math and science are also able to function professionally in another language.

It is also possible that international assessments do not capture characteristics of American schooling that may be very important in a global knowledge and innovation economy, especially the encouragement of creativity, independence of thought, and a wide range of talents through a broad curriculum and menu of extracurricular activities (Zhao,

2009). The breadth of the American school curriculum is traditionally one of its strengths (although the increase in high-stakes testing of a limited range of subjects is reducing that breadth). Clearly, international assessments do not measure everything. However, those areas they do measure—reading, math, and science—are certainly critical indicators of the quality of an education system. The PISA tests, in particular, are constructed to measure the kind of problem-solving and application skills that are essential to creativity and are increasingly being called for by educators, policymakers, and the business community.

What can we learn from international comparisons? Parents, teachers, and education policymakers are looking for information on how well schools are preparing their students for life. Most countries have national data and reports, such as the National Assessment of Educational Progress (NAEP), which allow states, for example, to compare the performance of their schools with other states. But international comparisons enable us to look at educational performance in a much broader context. In the past, such comparisons were largely of interest to academics, but the advent of a global knowledge economy has given us a critical "need to know." Today, PISA results show what is possible in education: that countries can achieve both excellence and equity. The repeated administration of these tests and the development of large-scale databases over time also allow us to see that significant change is possible and enable countries to gauge their progress against the most successful education systems in the world. Finally, they enable us to consider a wider range of policy options against a broader base of evidence as to "what works."

Countries also face common challenges. Societies everywhere are becoming more heterogeneous. And as skill sets change and people press for greater opportunities, governments everywhere experience similar difficulties in increasing quality, effectiveness, and accountability. There is a rich conversation to be had about approaches to new challenges. Other sectors of American life routinely study international trends in their fields; it is surprising that U.S. education has not been informed by international experience.

## The High Cost of Low Educational Outcomes

How much impact does the educational quality of a nation's schools have on economic prosperity? This is a key question. Some people argue that the relationship is not that important, pointing out that despite the United States' mediocre performance on international tests since *A Nation at Risk* was published in the early 1980s (National Commission on Excellence in Education, 1983), the nation has still prospered economically. Although true in some respects, what this argument doesn't take into account is the time lag between the population's education levels and the country's economic output. In other words, America still enjoys a higher proportion of older adult workers with high school and college diplomas than its international counterparts. We have not yet seen the impact of a U.S. workforce that is less well educated than that of many other countries. Certainly, a nation's economic growth is influenced by more than its educational level, and the United States has a favorable economic climate in many other areas. Despite the excessive risk taking of American banks that led to the financial crisis of 2008, the United States' legal and financial systems, large supply of capital, research and technologies companies, and culture of entrepreneurialism are second to none and can, to some extent, compensate for a weaker K–12 education system. The United States is ranked fourth in the World Economic Forum's 2010–2011 Global Competitiveness Index precisely because of these factors (Schwab, 2010). However, the global competitiveness report also notes that America's costly but unproductive education and health systems constitute threats to its competitiveness and a reason for companies not to locate here. And despite the fact that the U.S. economy has grown overall in the last two decades, large sectors of the economy have moved to other parts of the world, where companies find not only cheaper labor but increasingly highly educated knowledge workers.

If the cost to society is significant, the monetary cost to an individual student of low educational performance is also extremely high. A high school dropout in 2005 had an average annual income of $17,299. If that student had graduated, he or she would have earned $26,933—a difference of $9,634. Having an associate's degree raised the average income to $36,645, and a bachelor's degree brought in $52,671 (U.S. Census Bureau, 2006).

High school graduates also contribute more to the society through their increased purchasing power and taxes. They are less likely to become teen parents, they raise healthier children, and they are less likely to be in prison or rely on government food or housing programs. Dropouts not only earn less but also are more likely to be unemployed. In the 2009 recession, the rate of unemployment for dropouts was 15.4 percent, compared with 9.4 percent for high school graduates and 4.7 percent for college graduates (U.S. Bureau of Labor Statistics, 2009). Princeton University researcher Cecelia Rouse calculated that each dropout costs society $260,000 (Rouse, 2005). If you multiply the number of dropouts by that amount over a 10-year period, the cost to society is on the order of $3 trillion (Alliance for Excellent Education, 2009). That is one measure of the economic cost of the United States' low global ranking in high school graduation rates.

There are economic costs and benefits not only to the amount of education, as measured by high school and college graduation rates, but also to the quality of education. Drawing on research conducted over the past 10 years on why some countries have succeeded economically while others have not, the Hoover Institution's Eric Hanushek and the University of Munich's Ludger Woessman used economic modeling to relate cognitive skills as measured by PISA and other international assessments to economic growth of OECD countries. Their analysis showed that relatively small improvements in the skills of a nation's workforce can have a large impact. For example, if all OECD countries boosted their PISA scores by 25 points over the next 20 years, a growth surpassed by Poland between 2000 and 2006, there would be an aggregate gain of $115 trillion over the lifetime of the generation born in 2010. Bringing all countries to the average performance of Finland, one of the consistently top-performing countries on PISA, would result in gains of about $260 trillion (OECD, 2010a). This analysis also showed that it is the quality of learning outcomes, not the length of schooling, that makes the difference.

Naturally, there is uncertainty in these projections, and there are lively disagreements among economists about how to do economic modeling. However, even if these projected benefits are reduced to minimal estimates, the reports indicate that the costs of improving schools would be more than paid for by future economic growth. In the economies of the past, which were based on raw materials, primary production, or manufacturing, the role of human capital was less important. But in today's knowledge-based economies, human capital is a critical ingredient in economic growth, productivity, and innovation.

## The Need to Become World-Class

For most of the second half of the 20th century, Americans believed— and rightly so—that ours was the best education system in the world. But the concern that the United States is losing its edge has been growing steadily more urgent. The warning salvo fired by *A Nation at Risk,* with its famous threat of the "rising tide of mediocrity," has grown to a barrage of unease in reports like *Rising Above the Gathering Storm* (National Academy of Sciences, 2005), which argues that the United States is losing its lead in science, and *Tough Choices or Tough Times* (National Center on Education and the Economy, 2007), which argues that the U.S. standard of living will fall without radical reforms to increase educational performance and innovation; books by individual scholars like Linda Darling-Hammond (2010a), which make the case that America must seriously commit to equity to succeed in the "flat" world; and films like *2 Million Minutes,* written by software entrepreneur Bob Compton, which focuses on the ambition and hard work of Indian and Chinese high school students. This issue weighs heavily on the minds of parents, too, who wonder if the United States can maintain an educational system and economy that will allow their children to have a good standard of living in a world that is completely transformed from the world in which they grew up.

Reflecting this escalating concern about the need for dramatic improvement in U.S. education, President Barack Obama said, "In a 21st century world, where jobs can be shipped wherever there's an Internet connection, where a child born in Dallas is now competing with a child in New Delhi, where your best job qualification is not what you do, but what you know, education is no longer just a pathway to success; it's a prerequisite for success" (Obama, 2009). Arguing that the No Child Left Behind legislation, with its emphasis on closing achievement gaps in basic skills, was not ambitious enough, he went on to call for the development of a "world-class education system," reducing the high school dropout rate, and once again making the United States first in the world in college graduation rates.

A world-class education system should not just be defined by rates of high school and college graduation but also by the quality of its educational outcomes and whether the content and skills are adequately preparing students for a rapidly changing global environment. The education system in the United States has many strengths that should not be underestimated, but it also has major weaknesses. We cannot afford to rest on our past educational accomplishments. Over the past two decades, tectonic shifts have occurred in the economic and educational landscape of the world. The global context has changed, global educational standards have changed, and the skills needed to be successful in the global knowledge economy have changed. But while the world has altered so dramatically, our schools have not. Just as a market leader in the corporate world can get eclipsed by newer companies, the American school system has been overtaken in many areas. The future of the economy, jobs, and other national challenges is always unpredictable, but a good education is the best tool we have to prepare the next generation of Americans for the rapidly changing world.

The next chapter looks at how a number of countries, selected from many different parts of the globe, have successfully developed education systems that outperform the United States and produce more equitable outcomes at lower cost. It also considers the challenges that face these systems and presents takeaway lessons for American educators.

# 2

# SUCCESS STORIES FROM AROUND THE WORLD

In this world, the optimists have it . . . not because they are always right but because they are positive. Even when wrong, they are positive, and that is the way of achievement, correction, improvement, and success.
**—David Landes**

Some people travel the world to sit on beaches, others to see historical monuments or art museums or sporting events. I like to visit schools. Schools are microcosms of the societies they serve. Through them, you can see the struggles of the past and the tensions of the present but also glimpse immense hopes for the future. In the 21st century, the desire of families and governments everywhere, poor as well as rich, is for children to get a good education.

Schools come in all shapes and sizes. In many parts of the world, especially in Africa and South Asia, school buildings are very basic—simple buildings and roofs with mud or concrete floors and battered secondhand desks, if there are desks at all. At the other extreme, you'll find schools that feature gleaming new buildings and look more like colleges. Full of the latest technology, they are modern showpieces of pride and ambition. Inside the world's school buildings, there is also enormous variety in the quality and style of education provided. In far too many schools in the poorer parts of the world, I have seen unimaginative rote learning where children sit in rows, copying from the blackboard or reciting from old books left by missionaries. But I have also seen innovative programs where dedicated educators or philanthropists are introducing problem solving and project-based learning into poor rural schools, or building science labs in elementary schools located in drug-infested slums. Heroic individuals who are making a difference in children's lives are everywhere. The challenge today is not how to cultivate a few effective classrooms or effective schools, but how to create effective *systems* of schools to bring high-quality education to *all* children.

The global knowledge economy is a game changer. All over the world—from Indonesia to Poland, India to Norway, South Africa to Brazil—countries have been improving the education system as a pathway to participation in that economy. In the past, education systems tended to be inward looking. Schools and education systems considered themselves to be unique and thought that differences in culture and political systems made policies and practices developed elsewhere irrelevant. But today, governments and educators everywhere are looking for innovations and ideas for how to improve their systems from wherever they can find them. They recognize that no single nation has all the answers to the educational challenges produced by this new knowledge and innovation economy, and a new global marketplace of educational ideas is therefore developing.

Many high-performing nations have, in fact, been systematically searching the world for improvement ideas for a long time. The United States has been an important source of these ideas because of its leading position in education in the mid–20th century, the scale of its research enterprise, and significant innovations in many aspects of K–12 and higher education. For example, the now-famous Singapore math curriculum was developed using analysis of math research from around the world but especially from the United States. The Chinese compulsory education law was modeled on those in the United States. In the post–World War II period, many European countries (including England, where I grew up) looked at American comprehensive high schools as a better way to promote equal educational opportunity than their own separate and highly unequal academic and vocational schools. And today, many countries seeking to make their economies more creative and innovation oriented are interested in the kinds of constructivist pedagogies employed in some U.S. schools. At the higher education level, the United States' top research universities and community colleges are being emulated in many parts of the world.

Perhaps because of the U.S. position as the world leader on education in the mid–20th century, American K–12 educators have not been very active participants in these international benchmarking activities until recently. But now that it is crystal clear that other systems have moved ahead of the United States in important respects, there is growing interest in understanding more about how school systems in other parts of the world have raised their achievement. In this chapter, I describe some countries and education systems that have moved or are moving from poor to good to great. My purpose is to identify the key factors that have enabled these countries to develop strong systems of schools that are setting the gold standard. I have deliberately selected systems—Singapore, Canada, Finland, Shanghai (China), and Australia—that differ greatly from one another but outperform the United States on international assessments, producing both excellence and equity at lower cost. For each country, I also suggest key lessons for U.S. educators.

## Singapore: Using Education to Jump from the Third World to the First

When Singapore became an independent nation in 1965, it was a poor, small, tropical island with few natural resources, little fresh water, rapid population growth, substandard housing, and recurring conflict among the ethnic and religious groups that made up its population. At that time, there was no compulsory education and only a small number of high school and college graduates and skilled workers. Today, visitors to Singapore see a gleaming global hub of trade, finance, and technology. The country is one of Asia's great success stories—a transformation from third-world status to first-world status in two generations.

Singapore's students are also consistently high performers on international assessments, having placed first in the world in math and science on the TIMSS studies of 1995, 1999, and 2003, and second in math, fourth in science, and fifth in reading on PISA assessments in 2009. How did this "little red dot on the map," as Singaporeans frequently refer to their country—a nation that is not even 50 years old—transform itself into a global economic and educational leader in such a short period of time? The answer hinges fundamentally on its education system. Lacking other resources, this island republic viewed human capital as its most precious asset. The Singapore government saw education as central to building both the economy and a sense of nationhood. Over a 40-year period, Singapore has been able to raise its education level from one similar to that of many undeveloped countries to one comparable to the best in the OECD (Stewart, 2011b). Naturally, the current Singapore school system did not emerge full-blown, but rather developed along with the economy in three broad phases.

## Phase 1: Survival (1959–1978)

During the first phase of Singapore's educational journey, now known as the survival phase, when most of the population was illiterate and unskilled, the government focused on expanding basic education as quickly as possible. Schools were built rapidly, people were recruited to staff them on a wide scale, established schools run by different ethnic (Chinese, Malay, Indian) and religious (Muslim, Buddhist, Hindu, Christian, Taoist) groups were merged into a single Singaporean system, and a bilingual policy was introduced so that all children would learn both their own language and English. The expansion was so rapid that universal primary and lower secondary education was attained by the early 1970s. During this phase, Singapore's economy relied largely on the activities of its strategically located deep-water port and on attracting low-skilled, labor-intensive foreign factories (Lee, Goh, Fredriksen, & Tan, 2008).

However, the schools in this first phase were not of high quality. Large numbers of students dropped out, and standards were low. Over time, increasing competition from other countries in Asia for these low-skilled industries led to a growing realization by the government that Singapore's comparative advantage was eroding, and that it needed to transition to a higher-skill economy.

## Phase 2: Efficiency (1978–1996)

The watershed *Report on the Ministry of Education* (Goh, 1979), informally known as "the Goh report," highlighted the high dropout rates and low standards of Singapore's education system and led to the second phase of educational development, now known as the efficiency phase.

The government's economic strategy was to move Singapore from a third-league, labor-intensive economy to a second-league, capital- and skill-intensive economy. A new education system was introduced in 1979, moving the country away from a one-size-fits-all approach to schooling and creating multiple pathways for students in order to reduce the dropout rate, improve the quality of education, and produce the more technically skilled labor force needed for the new economic goals. Streaming (a form of tracking) was introduced, starting in elementary school, along with three different types of high schools—academic and polytechnic high schools that could lead to college, and technical institutes that focused on occupational and technical training. The Singapore Curriculum Development Institute was also created to produce high-quality curricula and inexpensive textbooks for the new system. Streaming was unpopular when it was introduced, but the package of reforms significantly reduced the dropout rate and raised the pass rate on the English O-level examinations (taken toward the end of secondary school). And by 1995, Singapore led the world in math and science TIMSS scores.

A major focus of this period was on the production of technically trained people at all levels. For example, Singapore invested significantly in a postsecondary Institute for Technical Education (ITE) for those who left school after grade 10 and for adult job changers. Today, ITE's facilities and equipment are comparable to a modern high-tech university, and close working relationships with industries in each sector keep it current with changing demands and new technologies. ITE's strong curriculum allows interested graduates to go on to polytechnics and universities as well as directly into industry. As a result of these changes, the image and attractiveness of vocational education greatly improved, and there has been strong market demand for ITE graduates.

## World-Class Vocational Education in Singapore: The Institute for Technical Education

In many countries, technical education is looked down upon as a dead-end option, out of step with the changing needs of employers. But vocational education has been an important part of Singapore's journey to educational excellence. In 1992, Singapore took a hard look at its poorly regarded vocational education program and decided to transform and reposition it so that it was not viewed as a path of last resort. Dr. Law Song Seng led the development of the Institute for Technical Education, with the goal of making the school "a world-class postsecondary educational institution" that is "recognized locally and internationally for its relevance, quality, and value in a global economy" (Lee et al., 2008, p. 122). His team revamped the curriculum and workforce certification system, developed courses in new industries, and consolidated existing technical institutions into three mega-campuses. When I visited the ITE with a delegation from the North Carolina Board of Education, we were impressed with the quality of the facilities, which were comparable to well-endowed American universities that any student or parent would be proud to be associated with. Every course has close ties to its industry, including the most modern multinational corporations. This keeps the courses up-to-date, the equipment modern, the internships readily available, and the path to jobs relatively smooth. To combat societal prejudice against less-academically inclined students, the ITE carried out a marketing campaign for its "hands-on, minds-on, hearts-on" type of applied learning.

*continued*

World-Class Vocational Education in Singapore:
The Institute for Technical Education (*continued*)

The result has been a doubling of enrollment since 1995, and ITE students now constitute about 25 percent of the nation's post-secondary enrollment. In 2009, more than 82 percent of ITE graduates who completed their training were placed in jobs. Pay levels for ITE graduates have been strong, and the ITE is now seen by students as a legitimate pathway to a decent future. Part of the reason for the success of the technical education at ITE is that students get a strong academic foundation early in their academic careers in elementary and secondary education so that they can acquire the more sophisticated skills required by leading-edge employers. The ITE received the IBM Innovations Award in Transforming Government, given by the Ash Center at the Harvard Kennedy School, and has been recognized worldwide as a global leader in technical education.

## Phase 3: Global Knowledge (1990s–Present)

In the early 1990s, although Singapore's focus on efficiency had yielded good results, it became clear that the shift in the global economy meant that the prosperity of nations would increasingly be defined by the discovery and application of new ideas. The Singaporean government decided that they needed to make a fundamental shift in Singapore's education system and focus on innovation, creativity, and research. At the higher education level, they provided generous funding for research and endeavored to attract top scientists and scientific companies. Singapore universities have research partnerships with universities around the world in fields such as bioinformatics, information sciences, and medical technologies. In fact, more than 1 million foreign nationals work in Singapore.

At the same time, Singapore worked toward a new vision for their educational system: "Thinking Schools, Learning Nation." Its goal was "a school system that could develop creative thinking skills and lifelong learning passion and a national culture where learning and creativity flourish at every level of society" (Ng, 2008b, p. 6). The government undertook a wide range of initiatives over a number of years to implement this vision by providing more flexibility and choice for students through a broader range of courses and different types of schools, along with a major commitment to information and communication technology (ICT) as a facilitator of different kinds of learning. "We need a mountain range of excellence, not just one peak," said then–Minister of Education Tharman Shanmugaratnam (Lee et al., 2008, p. 21). A major investment was also made in upgrading the teaching profession: the government revamped career paths and incentives for teachers in order to attract top talent, made upgrades to teacher education through the National Institute of Education, and committed seriously to professional and career development in ways that are described in more detail in Chapter 4.

There were also major changes in school management. Instead of the former top-down system by which the Ministry of Education was in control, schools were organized into clusters and given more autonomy. The old school inspection system was scrapped and replaced by a school quality improvement model under which each school sets its own goals and annually assesses its progress on academic performance and a wide range of other indicators of a healthy school climate. Schools that perform exceptionally well are recognized as "schools of distinction." Greater autonomy for schools also led to an intense focus on identifying and developing highly effective school leaders.

Later—under the policy directive "teach less, learn more"—curriculum, pedagogical, and assessment changes opened up more "white space" in the curriculum and engaged students in deeper learning. A major investment was made in ICT to facilitate self-directed learning and place greater emphasis on project work. In my conversations with Ho Peng, director general of education in the Singapore Ministry of Education, she emphasized that the analysis that lay behind these reforms was that the Singapore education system had great strengths in its holding power (the dropout rate from its 10 years of general education is less than 2 percent) as well as rigorous literacy, math, and science curricula, but it was too overloaded with content and needed to do more to promote the kinds of broad inquiry orientation that would enable future learning. To this end, art and music are being emphasized more in the curriculum, and elementary schools are putting more emphasis on play and on stimulating student curiosity.

## Victoria School: A Thinking School in a Learning Nation

Victoria School is one of the oldest schools in Singapore, tracing its origins back to an English class in Kampong Glam Malay School in 1876. It is a top school, winner of one of the Ministry of Education's Schools of Distinction awards. Founded as a boys' school with a strong tradition of sport and leadership development, its principal, Mr. Low Eng Teong, described to me how the school is trying to change its model of teaching and learning using the ideas developed by Howard Gardner in Project Zero (see www.pz.harvard.edu) and incorporating technology throughout the curriculum.

In a lower secondary art class, students sit at computers. In the previous lesson they had studied self-portraits by artists Affandi and Van Gogh and explored how these artists had expressed their emotions using contrasting colors and fluid lines. Now the students are learning skills in graphic design by creating self-portraits using different kinds of typefaces. They are also using the Teaching for Understanding framework to explore the concept of identity and how it can be harnessed and expressed in many different ways and from different perspectives.

In a nearby geography classroom, students study the different rates of economic and social development of various countries. Sitting at round tables, with laptops in front of them, students work together to examine development indicators such as adult literacy

rates, gross domestic product, employment structure, urbanization, and infant mortality rate for each of the four countries they
have been assigned; to assess the value of each indicator; and to
make a plan for what can be done to improve the development of
each country. The teacher roams the classroom, asking each group
probing questions about their conclusions thus far. Each group of
students then presents their conclusions to the class using Google
slides, while other students assess the presenting group's information and arguments using a rubric.

These classrooms don't fit the image of a traditional Asian classroom. Victoria School is in the vanguard of a change that Singapore
is promoting to "touch the hearts and engage the minds of learners by promoting a different learning paradigm . . . emphasizing
discovery through experiences, differentiated teaching, learning of
lifelong skills, and the building of character through innovative and
effective teaching approaches" (Ho Peng, Director General, Ministry
of Education, personal interview, August 2010).

## Key Success Factors for Singapore

**Vision and leadership.** Singapore leaders had a bold, long-term
vision of the role education should play in their country. Being a small
nation that has to compete in a fast-changing world with nearby larger
countries like China and India created a sense of urgency about the need
to build up the only resource Singapore had—human capital. The strong
link between education and economic development, and the value
placed on creating a socially cohesive society, has kept investment in
education a high priority. The economic imperative led to a focus on
developing high-quality math and science as well as to globally recognized vocational and technical education, an area where most countries
fail. It has also kept education dynamic and open to change as economic
conditions change, rather than being tied to the past.

**Commitment to meritocracy.** The education system that was in place during Singapore's colonial period was only for the elite and was segregated by ethnicity and religion. An early decision of the new republic was to replace that system with a universal state-funded system in which talent and hard work would prevail. Over time, the Ministry of Education has developed a range of polices to promote equal opportunity, including community support programs, early intervention programs in school, and multiple pathways to further education and careers. The success of these efforts in closing the achievement gaps among groups and creating an education system and society that is open to talent from wherever it comes has created the belief in the general population that education is the route to advancement and that hard work pays off for students of all ethnic backgrounds and all ranges of ability.

**Ambitious standards.** Rigor is the watchword of the Singapore education system. Its primary school leaving exam and Singapore's own O- and A-level standards are as high as anywhere in the world, and students work hard toward achieving these milestones. In addition, all students have a strong early foundation in the core subjects of math, science, and literacy in two languages, which sets them in good stead for whichever education and career path they choose.

**Curriculum, instruction, and assessment system.** Singapore does not just establish high standards and then assume that teachers will figure out how to achieve them. Its Curriculum Development Institute has produced high-quality curricula in math, science, technical education, and languages that teachers are well trained to teach (Hong, Mei, & Lim, 2009). Other countries are now benchmarking their curricula against Singapore's (Ginsberg et al., 2005).

**High-quality teachers and principals.** In the past, Singapore had teacher shortages and was not always able to attract high-quality workers into the profession. In the 1990s, the Ministry of Education developed a comprehensive human resource system designed to draw the high caliber of teachers and school leaders needed to meet the country's ambitions for its students. This system includes active attention to recruitment of talent, coherent training, and dedicated, ongoing support. Singapore's human resource management system, perhaps the best in the world, is described in more detail in Chapter 4. Today, education policies in Singapore are focused less on structure and more on maintaining and increasing the quality of the education profession.

**Alignment and coherence.** In many countries, there is an enormous gap between policies and their implementation at the school level. In Singapore, there is enormous attention to policy planning and to the details of implementation. Whenever a new policy is developed, the Ministry of Education, the National Institute of Education, cluster superintendents, principals, and teachers all work through how to bring the policy about and assess whether it works. The result is very strong fidelity of implementation and relatively little variation among schools.

**Accountability.** Singapore uses *performance management* to drive improvement. Teachers, principals, university faculty, and Ministry of Education officials all have incentives to work hard, and a sophisticated performance evaluation system, using multiple measures and multiple reviewers, links performance to career development. This is described further in Chapter 4.

**Global and future orientation.** Singapore's education system has benefited from focused use of international benchmarking, studying aspects of many other systems and then adapting them to the circumstances of Singapore. More recently, it has also made a significant commitment to research on classroom pedagogy as part of its culture of continuous improvement. This is an education system that recognizes that the world is changing very rapidly—and one that demonstrates the capacity to learn and adapt. Singapore fosters a global outlook for everyone; teachers, principals, and students are expected to have "global awareness and cross-cultural skills" and to be "future-ready" (Singapore Ministry of Education, 2010).

## Challenges for Singapore

The features described above have helped to make Singapore's education system world-class, but no system can rest on its laurels, and Singapore educators are certainly not complacent. Because it is a tiny country, Singapore is always vulnerable to the actions of larger powers.

Through a wide range of initiatives, the education system is trying to respond to the perceived need for creative and flexible workers in a 21st century economy. However, it is a considerable challenge to alter a traditional, content-heavy, curriculum knowledge transmission system that is reinforced by high-stakes examinations that parents believe in and support through extensive tutoring. It is also difficult for teachers who were raised with teacher-dominated pedagogy to fundamentally change their practice. Finally, the economic forces in the global knowledge economy are increasing the levels of inequality in all societies. Singapore has closed achievement gaps among ethnic and income groups to an amazing degree and focused on a high-quality education for those at the bottom as well as the top, but there is still work to be done. However, the way in which Singapore has created a world-class economy fueled by a world-class education system through a steady succession of quality improvements, considered policy decisions, and careful implementation is a major global success story.

## Takeaways for U.S. Educators

What can we learn from Singapore? Singapore is a small, highly centralized island state that was run by a single leader for 30 years. Changing the education system in Singapore is therefore easier—like "turning around a kayak rather than a battleship," according to Professor Lee Sing Kong, dean of the National Institute of Education (personal interview, 2010). But Singapore's student population of 522,000 in 360 schools is roughly the same as that of the state of Kentucky or a number of large American cities, suggesting that the types of major improvements brought about there could be undertaken at a state or city level.

From Singapore's beginning, there has been a very clear and persistent vision of the importance of education to economic development and social cohesion. The tightness of the link between education and economic development would not work in the U.S. context, but stronger collaboration among education, businesses, and economic leaders to cultivate a strategy for success in this new global context would create an urgent, forward-looking, and global focus on education development.

Singapore is also a good example of a continuous improvement system. No education policy change is taken on without careful consultation with schools as to how to make it work on the front lines. The voices of teachers and principals are integral to policy developments in Singapore. And all the key elements—curriculum, assessment, teacher training, professional development, and community support—are aligned to work together. Again, Singapore is a small and "tightly coupled" system, and different mechanisms would be needed in the larger, more multilayered U.S. system, but significant results in the classroom cannot be achieved without aligning all of these factors. This could be done at a state or city level.

Singapore has also made the development of high-quality educators—from the capable Ministry of Education staff to teachers and principals—a cornerstone of its system. Other countries are studying its human resource management system as well as its strong curriculum, especially in math, science, and technical education. There is one final lesson from Singapore's global and future orientation: in today's world, you have to be able to adapt rapidly to thrive!

## Canada: Increasing Achievement in Urban and Rural Schools

Canada's education system has many similarities to that of the United States, such as the structure of schools, with elementary, junior high, and high schools; a population encompassing a majority and significant minority populations, including indigenous and immigrant groups; and decentralized educational governance—even more decentralized than our own. In Canada, education is the responsibility of the 10 provinces and 3 territories rather than the federal government. However, unlike the United States, Canada is a consistently high performer on international assessments, ranking in the top 10 in math, science, and reading in the 2009 PISA assessments. Furthermore, over the past few years, several provinces have made significant efforts to raise their achievement and reduce the number of high school dropouts. Two strikingly different provinces, Alberta and Ontario, have achieved notable success.

## Alberta

Alberta is a prairie province of 3.5 million people. It is comparable in size and cultural background to Iowa, and it has a similar number of students in grades K–12— 589,000 students compared with about 515,000 in Iowa in 2008 (Fandel, 2008), and about the same percentage of students living in poverty. Alberta does have a larger share of students learning to speak English. However, students in Alberta perform significantly higher by international standards than students in Iowa do.

The province, growing due to its energy resources (oil and gas), has been investing in developing a high-quality public education system. According to the Canadian government, which estimates the average PISA scores of each province, Alberta ranked second only to Finland in science in the 2006 PISA, whereas the United States was ranked 29th. (The United States draws only a national sample for the PISA surveys rather than a state-by-state sample, so it is not possible to directly compare states with each other or with provinces in other countries.) When asked to explain why an already high-performing province was doubling its efforts, Alberta Minister of Education Dave Hancock said, "We are in a time frame where we don't know what the jobs will be in 10 or 15 years. With technology and the universal availability of knowledge and data, the learning has to move to how students can use data, can analyze and do problem solving. That changes the dynamic of how we learn significantly and so our system has to adapt" (Fandel, 2008, p. 70).

As part of its reforms, Alberta has put in place a provincewide K–12 curriculum in every subject, not just reading and math, so that all students have access to the same strong academic foundation. The curriculum is considerably more detailed than the kinds of guidance provided by the curriculum documents of many American states. For example, the science curriculum for grades 7, 8, and 9 is 73 pages long, whereas the Iowa core curriculum for middle school science is 4 pages long (Fandel, 2008). The curriculum is used by all Alberta schools and is credited with promoting greater consistency of instruction across the province. For example, Alberta had only 6.1 percent of its students scoring at the lowest level and 18.4 percent scoring at the top levels on the PISA science test in 2006; the United States had 24 percent scoring at the lowest level and 9 percent at the top levels. Teachers are involved in developing and assessing the provincial curriculum and have a great deal of freedom as to how they deliver it. The new social studies curriculum is also infused with more global content and perspectives, with the goal of preparing students who will be, in the words of Marcus Hauf, a 12th grade social studies teacher in Edmonton, "equipped with the necessary skills to analyze contemporary issues, make sense of them in historical context and to think critically about what is happening in the world today" (Fandel, 2008, p. 60).

A second element that Albertans regard as critical to their success is their teacher force. Teachers in Canada are paid better than most teachers in the United States, and the good salary attracts relatively strong candidates to the profession. After 11 years in the classroom and 4 years of university education, a teacher in Edmonton, Alberta, earned nearly USD$81,000 in 2008, according to the Alberta Teachers' Association. In Des Moines, one of the better-paying districts in Iowa, a teacher with the same experience and education would have made about USD$49,000, according to the Des Moines Education Association (Fandel, 2008). This is true even though Canadian per-pupil expenditures for K–12 education are lower than in the United States: USD$7,837 in Canada in 2005 compared with USD$10,390 in the United States (OECD, 2008). The recent reforms have put a major emphasis on and invested resources into professional teacher development. Every teacher develops an annual professional growth plan, which has to be aligned with the goals of the school and the province curriculum, but teachers propose how to attain their goals.

An action research program has also been implemented, the Alberta School Improvement Scheme, through which groups of teachers in a school come together to introduce innovations in teaching and learning and in student engagement and study their impact. There is now a growing provincewide repository of projects, and an annual conference brings people together to share their findings and progress. This process has really helped to improve teachers' skills and their attitude toward and use of data (Alberta Initiative for School Improvement, n.d.).

An accountability system consisting of provincewide achievement tests in grades 3, 6, and 9 and a diploma examination in 12th grade complements the focus on curriculum and professional development. And school report cards present test results, high school completion rates, and other measures of engagement and performance determined in consultation with the local community. Thus, within its schools, Alberta has developed a culture of high expectations for student performance and an ethos of continuous improvement among its educators.

Despite the fact that Alberta is already high performing by international standards, the Alberta Ministry of Education is launching a new reform program focused on the skills needed in the 21st century. It is often hard to persuade people to change when a system is clearly successful. But recognizing that the province's natural resources may not last forever and that the economy needs to shift to one based on human resources, in the spring of 2010 the ministry launched an in-person and online public engagement initiative built around the question "What should the educated Albertan look like in 20 years?" The findings of the report, *Inspiring Change*, are now being turned into policies (Alberta Ministry of Education, 2010). In public forums and during his reading of the 2011 Education Act before Alberta's Legislative Assembly, Minister of Education Dave Hancock has noted, "It is our responsibility to educate our children for their future, not our past."

### Ontario

The story of education reform in Ontario, where 27 percent of students are immigrants, is of great relevance to American educators. Ontario is Canada's largest province, responsible for the education of 2 million students. Much of the large immigrant population lives in Toronto, which is one of the world's most diverse cities, with more than 125,000 immigrants arriving each year from dozens of different countries and language backgrounds. Ninety-five percent of Ontario's students are in public schools. The Ontario Ministry of Education governs four publicly funded school systems, since in Canada students may select Protestant or Catholic schools in either English or French.

In the 1990s, a Conservative provincial government raised standards, cut funding, introduced teacher testing, reduced professional development, and increased support for private schools. The result was a period of intense labor unrest and strikes, strong public criticism of schools, high teacher turnover, and some flight to private schools. In 2004, a new premier and provincial government were elected with the goal of increasing achievement, bringing peace to labor relations, and increasing public confidence in the schools. The government introduced a set of reforms focused on increasing literacy, numeracy, and high school graduation rates (Asia Society & Council of Chief State School Officers, 2010). Just as important, they created the Ontario Education Partnership Table, where all the stakeholders in the system came together to create a new political consensus and work out how to achieve these goals.

---

### Bringing Government and Unions Together in Ontario: Results Without Rancor or Ranking

For almost a decade in the 1990s, a Conservative party government in Ontario had enacted education reform efforts while battling with the teachers' unions. The government cut funding, reduced professional development, introduced teacher testing, and took out television ads that blamed teachers for the failings of schools. There was considerable public dissatisfaction, poor morale among teachers, several years of teacher strikes, and no improvement in student performance.

Then, in 2004, a new provincial government headed by Dalton McGuinty took office and dramatically changed the approach to education reform. The government reached out to the teachers' union to restore trust and consulted with them on reform strategy and ways to make reform effective. They signed a four-year collective bargaining agreement. They spent time in schools listening to teachers. The government's literacy and numeracy reform strategy was based on the assumption that teachers wanted to do the right thing but lacked the tools and capacity to do it, and that reforms

*continued*

**Bringing Government and Unions Together in Ontario: Results Without Rancor or Ranking** (*continued*)

could not be successful unless teachers were respected and bought in to the reforms. The deputy minister met quarterly with the teachers' unions, superintendents, and principals' associations, and an Ontario Partnership Table was created to bring a wider range of stakeholders together two to four times a year. Working tables of smaller groups delved into more detailed issues in the implementation of reforms. The government abolished the hated teacher test and changed their approach to teacher effectiveness by promoting professional teacher development, which they saw as the single most important factor in the improvement of teacher quality and student achievement.

Two architects of the reforms, Michael Fullan of the University of Toronto, who served as Senior Advisor to the Premier, and Ben Levin, who served as Deputy Minister of Education during this period, termed the Ontario approach "results without rancor or ranking" (Levin, Glaze, & Fullan, 2008, p. 23).

With 5,000 schools and numerous school boards to deal with, the Ontario reformers picked a limited number of targets to try to achieve. They set specific targets: 75 percent of students achieving at the provincial standard (70 percent, or *B* grade) in literacy and mathematics in the 6th grade (age 12), and a secondary school graduation rate of 85 percent. The major strategy chosen to meet these targets was professional capacity building—in the provincial Ministry of Education itself, in district school boards, and in schools and classrooms. The strategy, which was based heavily on Michael Fullan's research into implementation of school change, was based on the premise that top-down reforms do not achieve lasting change because they are not typically focused on the instructional core, they assume that teachers know how to do things that they don't, schools are overwhelmed by too many reforms, or they do not achieve teacher buy-in. So reformers set about addressing all of these issues.

A separate unit was created in the Ministry of Education and staffed by excellent educators—not bureaucrats—to work on the Literacy and Numeracy Initiatives. Schools and districts were required to create teams to develop achievement targets and plans for meeting them. Within schools, there was extensive professional development for teachers focused on key instructional practices in literacy and numeracy. In elementary schools, thousands of new teaching positions were created and new art, music, and physical education teachers were added to enrich the curriculum and allow regular classroom teachers more professional learning time. Intensive assistance was provided to the schools that had the greatest difficulties (Levin et al., 2008).

At the high school level, the Student Success Initiative was based on the recognition that potential dropouts can be recognized by the 9th grade. Teams were created in each school to track data on which students were likely to drop out, and the ministry gave each district funds to hire a student success leader to coordinate district efforts as well as a student success officer in each school. A number of initiatives were created to keep potential dropouts engaged in school, including credit recovery programs and high-skills majors, developed with employers to provide up-to-date skills to students who were not engaged by the traditional high school curriculum.

Reflecting the new government's view that government and the teaching profession had to work collaboratively rather than combatively, Ontario's approach to teacher effectiveness also shifted from teacher testing to teacher development. They abolished the much-hated test for initial teachers and developed a new framework for teaching and leadership that included a universal new teacher induction program, a new competency-based teacher program, a new competency-based teacher performance appraisal system in conjunction with annual professional learning plans, and a new talent identification and leadership development system for principals that included new principal preparation, mentoring, and evaluation components (Pervin & Campbell, 2011).

By 2010, the reforms had increased the numbers of students achieving the 6th grade standard from 54 percent in 2004 to 68 percent and had increased high school graduation rates from 68 percent in 2004 to 79 percent in 2009. The reforms had also reduced the number of low-performing schools from 20 percent to under 5 percent, improved teacher morale, and reduced the attrition rate of new teachers by two-thirds (Levin, 2008).

### Key Success Factors in Canada

**Provincewide strategy.** Canada has shown that high-level performance can be driven from the province level (roughly equivalent to a U.S. state). In fact, Canada has no federal ministry or department of education. Within the provinces, there is also a complex system of local school boards, defined not only geographically but also by language and religion. Despite this local complexity, a number of Canadian provinces, including Alberta and Ontario, have been able to develop and implement significant provincewide quality improvements rather than improvements that affect only a small number of schools. One reason this is possible is the fact that over a number of years, financing of schools has moved from the local to the province level, which enables the provincial government to ensure that resources are distributed fairly and can also be used to create long-term reform programs, such as Alberta's broad provincewide curriculum or Ontario's focused literacy and numeracy effort. Information is broadly shared among provinces through a Council of Ministers and through universities, so that Canada performs well as a whole even though education is managed at the provincial and local levels.

**Collaboration with unions and other stakeholders.** The Ontario reforms began with the election of Dalton McGuinty as premier of Ontario, and his strong leadership has been critical. However, the antagonistic atmosphere that prevailed for a number of years prior to his election inspired a great need to reestablish trust between the government, the school boards, the teachers and the public. The creation of the Ontario Education Partnership Table brought together all the stakeholders two to four times a year; this collaborative working environment is key to the province's educational success.

**Focus on instructional content and capacity.** A key feature of Ontario's approach to reform has been professional capacity building, focused on classroom results, at the provincial, district, school, and classroom levels. A new Literacy and Numeracy Secretariat was created within the ministry (now called the Student Achievement Division); new types of positions (e.g., student success officers and literacy specialists) were created within schools, and leadership teams were created in each district; resources for professional learning about literacy and numeracy instruction were developed; and focused support was provided to unsuccessful schools. Thus, the strategy combined top-down policy prescription with bottom-up capacity building to produce results. Similarly, the Alberta system pairs a provincewide curriculum with a strong focus on professional development to build teachers' capacity.

**Approach to teacher effectiveness.** Overall, Canada has a good supply of teachers with enough well-qualified applicants, decent working conditions, and competitive salaries by international standards. In Ontario in the 1990s, the efforts to cut back expenditures, introduce teacher testing, roll back wages, and blame teachers for all the problems of the schools negatively affected teachers. They left the profession early, and Ontario struggled to attract new educators. Shifting the focus from teacher testing to teacher development through a comprehensive career framework for preparation, support, and evaluation of teachers and school leaders made a significant change for the better.

## Challenges for Canada

Alberta's education system performs at a very high level internationally, but it has certainly not solved all of its education problems. Its dropout rate is higher than Iowa's, for example. But by getting more consistency in the quality of what is taught and the quality of teachers, it is increasing its overall levels of achievement and reducing dropout rates. Ontario increased numeracy, literacy, and graduation rates; sharply reduced teacher attrition and early retirement rates; and increased public confidence in the schools in a relatively short period of time (2004–2007), but it has not yet achieved universal high school graduation. In addition, improvements in Ontario's test results are more significant in the area of basic skills than in the area of higher-order thinking, and the sheer number of educational initiatives proved confusing to schools. Still, the shift in public climate and the strengthening of the capacity of educators in the system at every level to improve instruction has set the stage for continuing improvement.

## Takeaways for U.S. Educators

The success of reforms in Alberta and Ontario shows what strong leadership at the state or city level can achieve, even without a major national initiative. These reforms also show that strategies may need to be flexible in response to a particular context. Alberta's approach encompassed a broad improvement across the whole system, whereas Ontario focused on more targeted outcomes in reading, math, and graduation rates—bringing up the bottom. They were both facilitated by the movement of school funding to the province level over the past few years.

In the United States' current political climate of strong public criticism of teachers, one of the most powerful lessons from Ontario is that building collaboration and buy-in with key stakeholders, especially teachers, through the education partnership table is critical to bringing about policy change and sustaining reform momentum. But even with good policies, there is often an "implementation gap" between policies and what happens in the classroom. Here, the use of data to track students who were potential dropouts so that they could be supported from 9th grade onward, and the efforts to create alignment and coherence among the reforms at school, district, and provincial levels are also of direct application to the multilayered education system in the United States. Finally, the key focus of both provinces, intensifying over time, has been the strengthening of teacher and leadership capacity in schools through universal higher standards in preparation, mentoring and induction, performance appraisal, and professional development. The reform leaders believe that change cannot be driven primarily through test-based accountability and that capacity building at the school level is fundamental to real improvement in the classroom.

## Finland: Taking the Professional Route to the Highest Performance in Europe

When you visit primary schools today in Finland, you will see small, well-equipped schools of a few hundred students, typically with small class sizes of 15 to 20 students, although they can have up to 30. Students, who enter school at age 7 after attending a state-funded, play-oriented preschool, are busy working in cooperative learning groups in the classroom or around the school on projects involving math problems or going to the library to check out more books. Each student reads at his or her own level, and there is little classwide instruction. The teacher is typically working with one student who needs more help while being open to questions from others who are working on projects, sometimes of their own design. From a very early age, students are encouraged to be creative, take risks, and solve problems that interest them. Special support teachers provide additional assistance to students who need it.

The atmosphere is relatively calm and peaceful, and students are engaged in their individual work. Students receive a free hot meal in the school every day, and health care is provided by the Finnish national health system. Because there are no external assessments until the high school leaving exam in grade 12, teachers and students are free to concentrate on learning rather than on test preparation. Teachers assess students through a mixture of diagnostic and performance tests that they create and provide feedback to parents primarily through descriptive material rather than rankings or other numerical measures. The school day is relatively short, as is the school year. This schedule allows time for the teachers to develop curricula and work with teachers in other schools to innovate and problem solve.

Schools have played a critical role in transforming Finland from a relatively poor timber- and agriculture-based economy to a modern technologically based economy, home to a huge telecommunications industry that includes Nokia, the largest mobile phone manufacturer in the world. Education has always been respected in Finland. However, in the 1960s, Finland had a tracked and low-achieving education system that performed well below the level of other European countries, including its Scandinavian neighbors. In 1970, only 40 percent of Finnish adults had obtained an upper secondary diploma.

However, by 2000, due to a series of thoughtful reforms, Finland had become a high-achieving country, as measured by PISA assessments. It remained in the top group of countries in the PISA assessments of 2003, 2006, and 2009. In fact, in 2009, Finland ranked second in science, fifth in math, and third in reading—the only European country in the top group. Even more remarkable than Finland's high standards are its very equitable outcomes: across the whole country, there is less than 5 percent variation in achievement scores among schools. Graduation rates are very high, with 99 percent of the population completing basic education at age 16, and three out of five Finns attending state-funded higher education institutions. This expansion and quality development have been achieved with expenditures that are moderate by international standards. How did Finland transform itself from a country with an undistinguished track record in education to one with a world-class system?

Because of its small size and geographic location, the history of Finland is one of resistance to large nearby empires—first Sweden and then Russia. This has contributed to a strong sense of Finnish identity and values and to a high regard for Finnish language literacy that is an important cultural underpinning of the country's educational efforts. But these factors did not, by themselves, produce a strong education system. In the 1950s, Finland was an agricultural society that had suffered devastating losses of life during World War II and had a very limited and highly unequal school system. Most Finns had only six years of basic education, and secondary schools were mostly private.

In the 1960s, there was a wave of popular demands for greater social and economic equality as well as extensive discussions of Finland's economic future and how it could move away from its heavy reliance on timber. After many years of debate and disagreement, the parliament created a new basic education system: a common comprehensive school for all students from grades 1 through 9. This common school was not just another school structure; it represented a dream of a society in which all students, no matter what their background or where they lived, would get the quality of education, social support, and health care that they deserved (Sahlberg, 2011). The common school was implemented very gradually throughout the country, taking over private schools and merging the public and private teachers' unions. To address the challenge of getting all students to meet the same high standards, a new national curriculum was developed over a five-year period by the Ministry of Education in a process that involved hundreds of teachers (Sahlberg, 2011).

One consequence of the development of the common school and national curriculum was the realization that to hold all children—rather than just the group that had traditionally gone to secondary school—to the high standards in the curriculum, Finland would need teachers with different kinds of knowledge and skills.

In 1979, teacher preparation was incorporated into universities, and eventually master's degrees were required of all licensed teachers, even primary school teachers. As the teacher preparation system evolved, teachers were expected to be involved in research, have strong peda-gogical content knowledge, be trained to diagnose students with learn-ing difficulties, and differentiate instruction based on learning needs. Over time, as the quality and training of teachers strengthened, the ministry devolved more and more responsibilities to local schools and teachers. This degree of trust and professional autonomy to teachers in turn made teaching much more attractive as a career. Today, teaching is a greatly admired profession in Finland, on a par with other professions. Only 1 in 10 applicants is accepted into programs to become a primary school teacher, for example. Applicants must go through two rounds of selection, the first based on their high school record and out-of-school accomplishments, and the second based on a written examination on assigned books on pedagogy, an observed clinical activity, and inter-views regarding teaching as a profession. These top candidates then complete a rigorous teacher education program supported by the government (Sahlberg, 2011).

## No Child Left Behind in Finland

Finnish educators believe that with early diagnosis and intervention, all students can achieve success in a regular classroom. A nested series of supports responds quickly to any signs that a student is falling behind. First, all teachers are trained in diagnosing student difficulties; if a student does not understand a particular area, the teacher will work with the student after school to make sure he or she grasps the key concepts. Thus, students' difficulties do not have to wait for an end-of-year exam to be detected and addressed. Second, this support from the classroom teacher is supplemented by a special teacher who has additional training in learning difficulties and is assigned to each school to work with students who need extra help catching up. Third, every school has a "pupils' care group," which includes the principal, special support teacher, school psychologist, and classroom teacher. This multidisciplinary team meets regularly to discuss how classrooms are progressing and can access a broader array of municipal services if a student needs support that is beyond the school's capacity to provide. In some schools, teachers stay with their students for more than a year, getting to know them well and taking deep responsibility for their learning. The final level of support for students is provided through the national health care system, which is tax supported and available free of charge to families (Grubb, 2007).

The combination of uniformly excellent teachers trained to diagnose learning difficulties, a strong focus on early intervention, and support personnel available in schools helps to produce highly consistent academic results across the country. Teachers also feel supported—they are not left alone to struggle with students in difficulty. Finland's success in international assessments is due to practices across all schools that minimize the gap between the bottom and the top in student achievement scores.

Another consequence of the development of the common school from grades 1 to 9 was an increasing demand for upper secondary school. A reform of the upper secondary system was instituted that abolished the traditional structure and created a much more flexible, modular system with more choice of both academic and vocational options, both of which can lead to postsecondary education. As a result, 43 percent of Finns in their 20s have completed tertiary education, the highest percentage in Europe.

In the 1980s, the Finnish government gave up central bureaucratic control of education and devolved responsibilities for improvement to the schools. The schools became the center of the action, with responsibility for curriculum, assessment, and innovations in teaching and learning, especially those that would prevent early school failure. Schools worked collaboratively in networks with other schools to pioneer improvements. Attention to cognitive science and new conceptions of knowledge and learning led to more attention to problem solving. In the primary years, a focus was put on following students' natural curiosity. The improvements in the schools and the professional quality and responsibility of the teachers contributed to a high level of trust among parents, political leaders, and the schools. There are no external assessments in the comprehensive school, only sample testing in grades 2 and 9 to provide information on the functioning of the system as a whole to the Ministry of Education.

In the 1990s, an outside threat forced changes in the education system. The collapse of the Soviet Union, the major market for Finland's products, together with a banking crisis led to 20 percent unemployment in Finland, double the rate of the 2008 recession in the United States. The government was forced to develop a new economic model. It joined the European Union and decided to put a major emphasis on research, innovation, and telecommunications. This accelerated the trend in schools toward a focus on creativity and problem solving, individualized learning, flexibility, and working in teams. For example, the math curriculum focuses on problem solving from the earliest grades. Students spend their time solving meaningful and realistic problems rather than doing repetitive exercises. This is made possible, in part, by strong literacy development—by grade 2, all students are reading well enough to handle word problems (Office for Standards in Education, Children's Services and Skills, 2010). Teachers can spend enough time on complex problems because of the lack of pressure of external tests. By lower secondary school, students are expected to take an active role in designing their own learning activities and to work individually and in teams; by upper secondary school, the Finnish school model has no grade structure and is more like a college, with each student designing an individualized program, starting courses at different times, and often able to include both academic and vocational courses. The curriculum is also more global, with all students expected to learn two languages besides Finnish. In a short period of time, Finland has become one of the world's hotspots for innovation and telecommunications. The proportion of Finns who work in research and development careers is now three times the OECD average.

## Key Success Factors for Finland

**Commitment to equity.** Finland's reform story is not a case where a single leader introduced a major reform program. Instead, the ideas that underlie Finland's high performance have developed over time through debate and the establishment of a broad societal consensus. Chief among these are a commitment to equity, represented by the development of an untracked common school; early intervention systems that prevent children from falling behind; and the broader health supports and social safety net of a welfare state. Achievement gaps among socioeconomic groups were large in the 1970s but have shrunk considerably. And by 2006, Finland's between-school variance on the PISA science assessment was only 5 percent, while the average between-school difference in OECD countries was 33 percent.

**Excellent teachers.** Of all of the elements of the Finnish system, the one that most observers inside and outside Finland credit with Finland's superior performance is its high-quality teaching force. Requiring a master's degree of all teachers (increasingly, many have higher degrees as well), making the profession highly selective, investing financially in teacher training, developing a rigorous research-based teacher preparation program, and giving teachers considerable authority and autonomy

## "Only Dead Fish Follow the Stream"

Pasi Sahlberg is a former math teacher and later World Bank official who has been deeply involved in Finnish education reforms. He contrasts the model of what he calls "the global education reform movement" (GERM) with the distinctive Finnish approach to reform. GERM draws its ideas from the corporate world and emphasizes a focus only on core subjects, competition among providers, standardization of curriculum, test-based accountability, and top-down direction, while the Finnish "professionalism" model emphasizes breadth of curriculum, collaboration between schools, attention to individual interests, creativity, trust-based accountability, and local school autonomy.

in schools have put teaching on a par with other professions and created a profession that is admired and trusted in Finland. Teachers can diagnose problems in their schools, apply evidence-based solutions, and analyze their impact.

**Broad and individualized curriculum.** The Finnish curriculum is broad and individualized, firmly based in child development and modern learning theory. Play-oriented preschool is followed by elementary school, where the focus is on encouraging students to follow their curiosity and work on real problems. Students are expected to take responsibility for their own learning from an early age. This emphasis on creativity and individual responsibility for learning has been reinforced as Finland's technology sector has grown. At the national level, the curriculum is a broad general statement of goals. Both detailed curriculum development and decisions about pedagogy have been devolved to schools and teachers. Teachers are responsible for assessing students' individual progress. While this creates some issues with comparability, Finns believe that the harms often associated with standardized testing—"narrowing of the curriculum, teaching to the test, manipulation of test results, and unhealthy competition among schools—can be more problematic" (Pasi Sahlberg, personal communication, 2010).

**Professional accountability.** Perhaps most surprising to observers from the United States is the fact that Finland has no external standardized testing until students take a high school exit exam at the end of grade 12. Corresponding with the lack of standardized tests is a lack of highly formal external accountability mechanisms. Finland abolished its school inspectorate some time ago, and the ministry's formal check on schools is limited to periodic sampling of student learning in grades 2 and 9. Parents trust teachers as professionals who know what is best for children in much the same way that parents in the United States trust pediatricians. Schools work together in networks to improve their teaching and learning, a practice that also helps to explain the very small differences between schools in performance.

## Challenges for Finland

One of the challenges for Finland, and for much of western Europe, is educating its growing immigrant population. Although immigrants currently make up only 3 percent of the total Finnish population, their numbers are increasing. Immigrants are concentrated in the capital, Helsinki, and represent 50 percent of the population in some Helsinki schools. Certainly Finland's health and social safety net and its child-centered system of early intervention and support should prove beneficial, but the population changes are too recent to know what the educational outcomes will be in the future.

Also, as with any high-performing nation, Finnish educators worry as to whether the policies that have succeeded up until now will continue to drive the country forward. They worry that complacency among parents and political leaders will motivate leaders to keep education as it is as opposed to always changing and improving. There is also the concern that in a context of tighter budgets, some of the things that have made Finnish education successful, like smaller class sizes or early intervention, might be affected. Finland's education changes were created out of a social commitment and a need for national survival. What is the big idea that will engage the passions of the entire population in the future?

## Takeaways for U.S. Educators

Today, Finland is often cited as a model for education in a knowledge society, and it is a magnet for school reformers all over the world. In 2009, when I visited with a group of American chief state school officers to study the Finnish teaching profession, there was a group of educators from China visiting a school at the same time to observe implementation of cooperative education and learn how to make school autonomy work. Educators who visit Finland are inspired by the system's commitment to meeting the needs of every child, its respect for and trust in teachers, the strong constructivist pedagogy, and the predictable quality of education; every school in Finland is an effective school.

Others question whether Finland is too small and homogeneous to be a useful comparison for the United States. While Finland does lack the social and ethnic diversity found in much of our country, its population size (5,326,000) is comparable to that of many U.S. states, and some of Finland's key practices, such as raising the standards for the teaching profession and classroom-based early intervention systems, could be replicated within an individual state.

There are also cultural differences between Finland and the United States. Finland is a nation of readers, with the highest library use rate in Europe and a value system that places a great deal of trust in public institutions. In addition, the United States does not follow a Nordic social welfare model, although the social support elements needed to help all children learn can be found in many of our community schools and neighborhood support projects.

Still, while many other countries are trying to improve their achievement by focusing on one or two subjects, standardizing curriculum, and driving performance with test-based accountability, Finland provides an alternative model to challenge our thinking—one that undergoes only light national direction, allows substantial school autonomy, implements a broad and individualized curriculum that emphasizes problem solving and a global outlook, and combines high challenge with high support. Finland guarantees the quality of its system upfront in the high standards for selection and training of teachers and then relies on the expertise and professional accountability of teachers who are knowledgeable and committed to their students. Finland has successfully built a competitive knowledge economy while maintaining a Nordic social welfare model. In the current U.S. situation of low and unequal performance by international standards and loud criticism of teachers and their unions, it is hard to imagine this model, based on a trust in the profession, working in the United States. But the Finnish system's quality of schools and teachers, its combination of high expectations and high support, and the level of engagement Finnish students demonstrate in their learning are ideals to which we might aspire.

## China: An Educational Giant Emerges from Cultural Revolution

Forty years ago, China's economy was primarily based on subsistence agriculture; today it is the largest manufacturer of solar panels in the world. Forty years ago, most Chinese lived in rural villages; today, the majority of Chinese live in cities. The rise of China is indeed one of the critical developments of the late 20th and early 21st century. China's astounding economic performance has been extensively reported. Far less widely known are the dramatic gains it has made in education in a relatively short period of time. Since the end of Mao's Cultural Revolution (1966–1976), during which conventional schools were closed, teachers were sent to the factories or the countryside to do manual labor, and anyone with an education was suspect, the People's Republic of China has committed itself to education as a central priority to develop its economy and raise its 1.3 billion citizens out of poverty.

The first step was to rebuild the education system from the ruins created by the Cultural Revolution. In the 1970s, the national government in Beijing wanted to massively expand basic education but lacked the resources to do so. So it encouraged provinces and local communities to create schools. Drawing on the traditional respect for education in Chinese culture, which dates back thousands of years, as well as a powerful desire for social progress through education, communities did so with great enthusiasm, and universal primary education was achieved very quickly (Cheng, 2010). In 1988, a compulsory education law requiring nine years of basic education was passed, and enrollment rates skyrocketed. Expansion of upper secondary education followed, focusing on both traditional academic schools and vocational schools to meet the needs of the growing manufacturing sector. In the late 1990s and early 21st century, higher education expanded dramatically—from 6 million students in 1998 to about 30 million students in 2009 (Yang in Asia Society, 2008b).

In just 30 years, China has virtually eliminated illiteracy, expanded nine years of basic education to every part of the country, and dramatically expanded the number of Chinese students enrolled in higher education, both at home and abroad. The People's Republic of China now runs the world's largest school system, serving 20 percent of the world's students (200 million in elementary and secondary education), with less than 10 percent of the world's GDP. The rapidity of this growth was achieved through a combination of government vision and investment and huge social demand for education. The government's 2020 plan for education, released in 2010, calls for universalizing preschool, raising the retention rate in the nine years of basic education to 95 percent, increasing upper secondary school (high school) enrollment rates to 90 percent, and redressing the significant disparities that have arisen as a result of the local financing of schools through expanding central government funding of poorer areas. China's education system is on the move.

While this rapid expansion of education on an unheard-of scale was the main focus of this period, there have also been efforts since the 1990s to improve the quality of education in China. Although funding for schools was substantially local, standards and curriculum were the province of the national Ministry of Education. After studying the curricula of more than 30 countries around the world, the Ministry of Education introduced a curriculum reform effort in 2001. It was piloted in a small number of provinces and then disseminated to other parts of the country in 2007. The Chinese curriculum has traditionally been very heavily focused on math and science, with a core of biology, chemistry, physics, algebra, and geometry required of all high school students. The new curriculum attempts to reduce the emphasis on disciplines, introduce more arts and humanities, move away from knowledge transmission and rote forms of learning to more participatory learning, and change the form of assessments to promote the kinds of "creative and problem-solving" skills thought to be appropriate for the 21st century global knowledge economy. In 2001, the teaching of English from 3rd grade on was introduced throughout China to ensure that Chinese students could engage with the world, following several decades of national isolation. Finally, China also promoted greater decentralization of some curriculum decisions to better meet local needs.

China is a vast and diverse country with very uneven levels of development and income, from the gleaming modern cities of the east coast to vast agricultural hinterlands. The heavy role of local efforts in the expansion of basic education led to large disparities in education quality, especially between urban and rural areas. The ministry is now devoting its efforts to reducing these disparities and promoting equal opportunity in education. These efforts include creating boarding schools in rural areas to overcome the problem of children living long distances from school, providing scholarships to encourage people in rural areas to go into teaching, abolishing textbook fees in rural areas, and implementing a vast, satellite-based distance learning network that enables master teachers to work with students and teachers in rural areas to improve the quality of instruction.

While the scale and speed of China's education expansion has been impressive, until now there has been no way to know how the quality of China's massive system compared with those in other parts of the world. But for the first time in 2009, a mainland province of China participated in the PISA. When the results were released, Shanghai students came on top of the PISA rankings in all three subjects—math, science, and reading.

The city of Shanghai is the commercial headquarters of China, its most international city, and a pioneer of education reforms; the province of Shanghai also includes some less developed and more rural areas.

The province has been at the forefront of efforts to broaden the curriculum in Chinese schools, encouraging electives to broaden subject matter choices for students and sponsoring inquiry-oriented extracurricular activities such as science, theater, and entrepreneurship clubs. It has tried to reduce pressure from examinations in elementary school by reducing the number of "key" schools (entered by examination at the end of primary or lower secondary schools) and moving toward a system of neighborhood schools. In recent years, its schools have included children of the millions of families who have migrated from rural areas to the city to look for work. Shanghai has developed a strategy for strengthening lower-performing schools by pairing stronger schools with weaker ones and urban schools with rural ones to help them improve. Teacher distribution policies also try to ensure that higher-grade (master) teachers are spread among schools. The province has also created its own higher education entrance examination (to replace the national university entrance examination dreaded by every Chinese student) with a broader curriculum focus and measures of problem-solving skills. Although Shanghai is the most advanced area in China—other parts of China have not yet achieved its level of economic or educational development—it is a harbinger of what might develop in many parts of China over the next 20 years.

It is important to note that while Shanghai published its PISA results, other provinces that have taken the PISA surveys as a way to benchmark their progress against the rest of the world have not publically released them. Hong Kong, which was a colony of Great Britain until 1997, when it returned to Chinese sovereignty under the "one country, two systems" political arrangement, has a separate and differently structured education system and has long been a top performer in PISA.

### Key Success Factors in China

**Bold, long-term vision for education.** Through its investment in education, China hopes to make the transition from an agricultural and low-wage manufacturing economy to a world leader in a range of fields. China's long-term goals include universal 12 years of education by 2020, 100 first-class universities, science parks to develop products from

## China's Roadmap to Becoming a Learning Society

In July 2010, Premier Hu Jintao formally issued China's National Plan for Medium and Long-Term Education Reform and Development, which was two years in the making and underwent several rounds of public comment (millions of comments were received via the Internet). Emphasizing that education is the driving force for future development in China, this blueprint for educational modernization aims to continue expanding education from preschool to university while also addressing some of the quality, equity, and management concerns that arose during the rapid educational expansion of the previous two decades. Some of the specific goals from 2010–2020 include the following:

- Universalize one year of preschool.
- Raise the graduation rate from nine years of basic education to 95 percent.
- Raise enrollments in upper secondary school to 90 percent.
- Reduce disparities in financing of schools and achieve more balanced development through expanded central government financing of poorer areas.
- Narrow the gap between "top" schools and weaker schools.
- Reduce the homework burden on students.
- Diversify the college entrance examination system.
- Increase higher education enrollment to 40 percent of the age cohort.
- Increase the number of world-class universities.

More information on the National Plan for Medium and Long-Term Reform and Development is available online from the Chinese Ministry of Education (2010).

university research, and a modernized curriculum aimed at developing students' creativity and ability to apply their knowledge, their skills in technology use, and proficiency in English. It has set its sights on not just mass education but on a world-class education.

**Rigorous standards and core curriculum, especially in math and science.** Like most East Asian countries, China emphasizes math and science far more than the United States does. This is implemented through rigorous national curriculum standards, strong subject matter preparation, and ongoing professional teacher development; specialized math and science teachers as early as 1st grade; and a strong societal emphasis on math and science, including in the university examination systems. As a result, both girls and boys do well in science.

**Coherent teacher development system.** Like other East Asian countries, China has a coherent system of ongoing teacher development, described in more detail in Chapter 4. Prospective teachers are well prepared in their subject areas and immersed in observing experienced teachers on a regular basis. Once teachers are hired, they take part in weekly professional development sessions led by the master teachers in their school. A career ladder provides salary incentives based on public teaching lessons, mentoring younger teachers, and publications.

**Strong cultural commitment to education.** Respect for education is deeply ingrained in Chinese history, going back to the Imperial Civil Service Examination system. This very meritocratic system lasted from 603 to 1905 and was open to anyone in China who could study the five Confucian classics. The examination system gave scholars a status above that of a warrior or merchant in Chinese culture and created the strong cultural belief that effort, not ability, determines success. Chinese students work much harder than American students. Not only is the school year longer, but students in China also spend countless hours studying outside school. Overall, students in China spend twice as many hours studying as their American counterparts, both to honor their families and to participate in the expanding opportunities that are open to those with a good education (Stewart & Singmaster, 2010).

**International orientation.** Chinese education leaders use international benchmarking to improve their system. From the expansion of early childhood education to the development of world-class universities and science parks, Chinese education leaders systematically study the effectiveness of other countries' approaches as a way to improve their own. As noted the recent major curriculum reforms are attempting to move China away from its traditional didactic classroom practices, with their heavy emphasis on memorization, to more Western approaches that incorporate inquiry methods and more student participation in classroom discussion. Perhaps surprisingly, given China's isolation from the world for many years, Chinese schools and students are more internationally oriented than most American schools. In addition to the mandate that all students learn English, Chinese schools teach world history and geography and actively pursue sister-school partnerships with schools around the world.

## Challenges for China

Despite its impressive educational developments, China faces difficult challenges as it seeks to turn its huge population from a burden into an asset. The government is making major efforts to address the rural-urban gap, as discussed, but the disparity among the more than half of Chinese citizens who live on less than USD$2 per day and the increasingly affluent cities is a major threat to China's peaceful development. Although the government is devoting enormous resources to addressing these disparities, in rural areas, teacher qualifications, facilities, student achievement, and access to upper secondary education all lag behind.

Another major challenge to the success of Chinese schools is the university entrance examination, which is controlled by the universities. Critics point out that the examination places undue emphasis on math, science, and the memorization of esoteric material. Academics in universities have opposed the curriculum reforms being implemented in schools as well as changes to the university examination system itself. They regard reforms as a "dumbing down" of the curriculum and examination. The ongoing tension between standards as conceived by university academics and standards as conceived by leaders in elementary and secondary education is familiar to American educators. The government is trying to reduce the influence of the examination by encouraging provinces to develop their own exams or to experiment with allowing some students to enter university by alternate routes. Still, the belief in examinations as the guarantor of meritocracy is very strong, which means that high schools are very exam focused and students spend many hours with tutors to prepare for exams (Zhao, 2009).

A third major challenge for China is capacity. As the country's educational system expands at breakneck speed, there are capacity issues at every level. For example, when the Ministry of Education made the decision to implement universal English language instruction in schools, it lacked the thousands of teachers needed to carry out the mandate. Also, because most Chinese teachers grew up in a didactic education system, they are less familiar with inquiry-oriented pedagogy, and overhauling the profession will take an enormous effort. Universities have expanded, but they do not yet employ enough well-trained faculty, the quality of many courses is not high, and there have been significant problems with graduate unemployment, especially in the eastern cities.

### Takeaways for U.S. Educators

China is so vast and diverse and is changing so rapidly that any statement about China is both true and untrue at the same time. It is simultaneously a third-world country and a first-world country. But China's determination to provide a middle-class standard of living, high education levels, and a research- and innovation-based economy for its vast population is apparent.

The quote "Let China sleep, for when she wakes, she will shake the world" is attributed to Napoleon in the 19th century; certainly, China's recent economic rise to become the globe's second-largest economy (and, one day, its largest) is shaking the world. China has huge economic, environmental, and political problems to solve, but it is stiffening the global competition for high-skill and high-wage jobs. The U.S. economic and educational system has many advantages that can be built on to create an innovation-oriented economy and society, but only if we take very seriously the challenge of building a world-class education system for all of our students.

The U.S.–China relationship will probably prove to be the most important relationship of the early part of the 21st century. Our curriculum has been very focused on the United States (and, to some extent, Europe), and our students know very little about China, a part of the world that will be such an important part of their future. We need to engage with China; our students need to know more about Chinese culture and language. Chinese language programs and school partnerships between the two countries are growing, but they are starting from a tiny base, and we need to accelerate them.

There is much to admire in Chinese educational practice, including the serious academic focus of schools and students' engagement with their studies. There are other aspects, such as the intense focus on the university entrance examination, the restrictions on subject choice for students, and the more didactic classrooms, that would not be welcome in the United States (and the Chinese themselves are trying to modify many of these aspects). The East Asian system of teacher support, in which every teacher follows a tradition of close teamwork, meeting regularly to improve their classroom skills and the curriculum, is something that is now being emulated in the West to reduce the isolation of teachers, and the success of Shanghai in raising the achievement of weaker schools by pairing them with stronger schools and involving some of the best teachers in those efforts is also beginning to gain international attention.

## Australia: A Federal System Embraces a National Program

While visiting the school attended by my brother's two daughters in Perth, West Australia, I was struck by how familiar everything felt. Although the school uniforms and the choice of netball as the girls' competitive sport was a reminder of Australia's heritage as a British colony ("Surrey removed 11 time zones," as one wag put it), most of the school seemed very American. With its warm, sunny climate, modern buildings, relaxed atmosphere, and rambunctious students, it could have been a school in California. In the past, the "white Australia" immigration policy kept the schools fairly homogeneous—with the exception of the aboriginal population—but now, with substantial immigration from Eastern and Southern Europe and from South and Southeast Asia, the roster of student names in the school sounded like a United Nations roll call. Technology was very much in evidence, and some students who lived in remote mining towns in the "bush" or "outback" took classes via distance learning. Australia's increasingly close relationship with the booming economies of Asia was also evident in the number of Asian students who were studying at the local universities and the number of Australian students studying Asian languages.

Australia is also, like the United States, a federal system; the country is made up of six states and two territories. It has been a relatively high-performer on international assessments for some time, and it scores significantly higher than the United States. On the 2000 PISA assessment, Australia was among the eight countries tied for second place in reading performance. However, an analysis of trends in PISA from 2000 to 2003 to 2006 showed a steady decline in Australia's reading performance relative to other high-performing countries, while some of the top performers like Finland and Korea raised their performance and other, lower-performing systems, such as Poland, raised their performance significantly to come close to Australia's. Besides declining overall quality, an analysis of performance in science on PISA in 2006 that sorted countries into high quality/high equity, high quality/low equity, low quality/high equity, and low quality/low equity showed that Australia had high quality but low equity. (By comparison, the United States has low quality and low equity.) What this means is that the social background of students predicts more of the differences in educational performance than in other countries and that, unlike in countries like Finland, for example, the variation in performance among schools is mostly attributable to the background of the students—that is, whom the schools enroll rather than what the school does.

Recognizing that other countries were not standing still and not wanting Australian students to have a lower-quality or less equitable education than other countries, Australia introduced major reforms in 2008 (McGaw, 2010). There had been a series of reform efforts in preceding years, primarily at the state level. Broad national goals and frameworks had been developed starting in 1989, but in 2008, the states and federal government came together to create a national curriculum that was historically unprecedented. The rationales were that in the 21st century, the educational needs of young Australians were similar across the country, that all jurisdictions could do better working together to improve quality and equity than they could separately, and that globalization and international competition required a rapid response to those educational needs. The vision of the Australian curriculum is "to equip young Australians with the skills, knowledge, understanding, and capacity to effectively engage with and prosper in society, compete in a globalised world and thrive in the information-rich workplaces of the future and to make such a curriculum accessible to all young Australians, regardless of their social or economic background or the school they attend" (Australian Curriculum, Assessment, and Reporting Authority, 2011, para. 2).

The Australian National Curriculum for grades K–12 will be introduced in three phases, starting with English, mathematics, science, and history in the first phase; followed by geography, foreign languages and the arts in the second; and ICT, design and technology, economics, civics and citizenship, and health and physical education in the third. The curriculum is being put together by committees of academics and teachers with opportunities for public comment at each stage. The committees looked at the curricula in other high-performing countries (e.g., Singapore and Finland in math) to ensure that Australia's curriculum would be world-class. The curriculum is built around disciplines but also gives attention to general capabilities, such as creativity, ethical behaviour, ICT literacy, intercultural understanding, literacy, numeracy, self-management, social competence, teamwork, and thinking skills (McGaw, 2010). It also incorporates cross-curriculum themes, such as indigenous perspectives, Asia and Australia's engagement with Asia, and commitment to sustainable living. While the curriculum is traditional in its organization around disciplines, it attempts to set standards comparable to the best-performing countries and to establish high expectations for *all* students. It also tries to reduce the amount of content in math and science to provide greater space for students to work in depth.

The curriculum is not intended to constitute the entire educational experience of Australian students; there is room for local additions. But it is deliberately designed to cover a broad swath of the curriculum and thus avoid the problem of curriculum reform efforts that focus just on math and reading, pushing aside other subjects to focus on those that are subject to accountability testing and hence narrowing the curriculum at a time when the world requires students to have broader horizons. The curriculum will be online, and a national digital resource collection linked to the curriculum is being created. Australia will also publish achievement standards and will collect and publish samples of student work to clarify the expectations of students.

The Australian Curriculum, Assessment, and Reporting Authority (ACARA) was created by the federal parliament in 2008 with the council of ministers for the states as the policy body. In addition to leading the development of a national curriculum, ACARA is responsible for monitoring the overall performance of the school system through a National Assessment of Literacy and Numeracy in grades 3, 5, 7, and 9. Periodic sample surveys will also be undertaken in science, civics and citizenship, ICT literacy, and other areas as the National Curriculum is developed and implemented. ACARA will continue to involve Australia with international assessments run by IEA and OECD as a way to benchmark its progress internationally.

Increasing transparency to the public is another major goal. To that end, a new website, MySchool (www.myschool.edu.au), was launched in early 2010 to provide information on over 10,000 schools. The site includes not only public schools but also independent and Catholic schools, as the latter two categories constitute a significant proportion of schools in Australia, especially at the secondary level. The site supplies school profiles and performance data with a major focus on a community socioeconomic index so that results can be compared for schools with similar populations instead of through league tables that reward schools with the most advantaged populations. The site aims to provide greater transparency for parents (information about the site will be available in 18 different languages), teachers, and school leaders so as to highlight schools from which others can learn and to stimulate improvement. The site also draws attention to the need to expand the number of students performing at the highest level as well as raise the performance of those at the bottom.

Accompanying this new national curriculum, monitoring, and reporting strategy was a doubling of federal funding to schools, targeting disadvantaged schools in particular. A new Australian Institute for Teaching and School Leadership (www.aitsl.edu.au) was also established in 2010 to raise standards for the profession.

---

### Australian Institute for Teaching and School Leadership

The mission of the Australian Institute for Teaching and School Leadership is to provide national leadership in promoting excellence in the profession of teaching and school leadership by doing the following:

- Developing rigorous national professional standards.
- Implementing a system of national accreditation based on the standards.
- Developing a national approach to the accreditation of preservice teacher education programs.
- Fostering high-quality professional development.
- Engaging with international research and innovation.
- Working with key stakeholders, including unions, business and school communities, and ACARA.

## Challenges for Australia

These Australian reforms are very new. It is therefore too soon to assess how successful they have been, especially given that there are many complex details of implementation still to be worked out—schools in different states have different entry dates, certification processes, data collection methods, and so on. It is too soon to know whether these reforms will retain the political consensus and fidelity of implementation needed to bring about a significant improvement in quality and equity. The monitoring and reporting aspects of the reforms will need to be accompanied by significant efforts to build capacity in lower-performing schools in order to succeed, as collecting data alone does not produce achievement gains. The reforms will also require a large professional development and teacher preparation effort to get teachers ready to teach the new curriculum. Whether Australia will put sufficient resources behind this needed capacity-building strategy has yet to be determined. Still, the Australian vision and direction is unmistakable—a world-class and 21st century curriculum for every child, no matter where he or she lives.

## Takeaways for U.S. Educators

Australia scores much higher than the United States in international assessments, yet the nation is making moves to take increasing international competition very seriously, aiming for world-class expectations of all its students. Like the United States, Australia is a federal system in which the states have had considerable autonomy. However, recognizing how rapidly the world is changing and globalizing, the states and federal government have come together in a bold move toward a more national (but not federally controlled) system, reckoning that the benefits of establishing uniform high expectations for all students and being able to implement them jointly in a speedy and cost-efficient way outweigh the losses in state autonomy.

In Australia, the assessment tail does not wag the education dog. Curriculum comes first, and the nation has embraced a broad one, having seen the effects of focusing accountability on one or two subjects, thereby distorting and narrowing the schooling experience.

Countries around the globe are making unprecedented changes to their traditional education systems to prepare their students for a radically different world. The high-performing systems that serve as examples in this chapter vary in size, culture, population, and economic base, yet all have made substantial progress in educational quality and equity. The next chapter will examine the common elements that cut across these diverse systems and have driven the improvements in achievement. It also provides reflection questions for educators to stimulate discussion as to how their district or state could achieve world-class standards of learning.

# 3

# THE COMMON ELEMENTS
# OF SUCCESSFUL SYSTEMS

They must often change who would be constant in happiness and wisdom.
**—Confucius**

Improving schools is hard work. Every year, school systems everywhere introduce myriad reforms—in curriculum or pedagogy, structure or governance, technology, and so on. The majority of these reforms fail to achieve the substantial changes that are really needed. Over the past 20 years, numerous reforms have been implemented in American schools, requiring significant investments of resources, yet overall school performance has remained essentially flat. Since the start of the effective schools research in the 1980s, we have learned a lot about which elements are most critical to creating effective schools—indeed, the United States has hundreds of excellent schools. The challenge now is to create effective *systems*. We must work on producing not just a relatively small number of effective schools but on improving thousands of them. The countries examined in Chapter 2 have all achieved this kind of success, bringing high-quality education to hundreds of thousands of students.

Each country's education journey is unique and continuing. The cultural traditions, demographic makeup, stage of economic development, and nature of the political system all influence the priority given to certain issues and the potential to bring about different kinds of change. On the other hand, as reported in Chapter 2, significant changes have been taking place in different parts of the world and across many different cultures and many different national and political systems. What are the commonalities in the successful efforts of countries to increase graduation rates, raise performance levels, and reduce achievement gaps? The following eight areas hold important lessons for U.S. educators to consider. While the examples are national ones, the lessons we can learn from them are applicable to those working at any level of an educational system—district, city, or state.

## Vision and Leadership

There are no quick fixes in education. However, the countries described in Chapter 2 have shown that substantial improvement over a 5- to 10-year period is possible. Major change cannot be brought about just from inside the education system, however hard people try. Schools are deeply intertwined with their societies and economies, and reform requires political and societal leadership that understands the centrality of investing in education to the region's economic development. Leadership must also have a sense of moral purpose about the need to deal with inequities and promote a more just society. In Finland, for example, education reforms were driven in the 1960s by a dream of greater equality, and later by an economic crisis that led the country to reinvent its economy through education. In Singapore, the government saw smart and evolving investment in human resources as the way to rise from third-world status to first-world status. And in China, the government has used educational expansion to raise millions of people out of poverty and has a long-term plan to remake China as a prosperous middle-class society based on education and research.

In fact, as the role of human resources and talent becomes ever more central in modern knowledge economies, increasing numbers of societies are recognizing that education is critical to their future economic prosperity. Countries as diverse as Poland, Germany, Indonesia, Brazil, and Norway are making major reforms and raising student achievement. Worldwide, there is growing public demand for education. Reforms are often started by a single strong leader. For this reason, the rapid turnover in political leadership in many jurisdictions, whether countries, states, or cities, makes sustaining the vision and reforms long enough to produce results (5 to 10 years) extremely difficult. One key lesson from the province of Ontario has been the importance of bringing together stakeholders to design reforms that would achieve enough buy-in from teachers, parents, school districts, and corporations to withstand challenges and changes in leadership. The Partnership Table brought together key stakeholders on a regular basis to monitor the progress of reforms and revise them if necessary to maintain forward momentum. In Finland, too, there have been painstaking, multiyear efforts to build consensus among the multiple Finnish political parties to support the steady ratcheting up of achievement over two decades, a consensus that was only finally solidified when Finland's success by international standards was proven.

The vision also needs to be broad enough to encompass the entire education system. Even though systems can only deal with a limited number of changes at a time, if one part of the system changes but others don't, reforms will not succeed. For example, if an effort is made to recruit high-quality teachers into the profession, but no improvement is made in the organization and leadership of schools, then the new recruits will leave. Leaders who advocate one or another "silver bullet" will not succeed.

Educational change is often precipitated by a crisis; certainly, the transformative changes brought about by the globalization of economies and the growth of educational excellence in many parts of the world has produced a "Sputnik" moment for the United States. The fact that the significant global economic growth is taking place *outside* the United States, and that there is increasing competition from well-educated people in formerly undeveloped countries, poses a challenge to American leadership and prosperity. President Obama has laid out a vision of increasing high school and college graduation rates and making U.S. education world-class. But given the multilayered system of education in the United States, the vision needs to be articulated by leaders at every level. It needs to include effective attention to bringing up bottom-level performance, since a major factor in poor U.S. performance on international assessments is the high proportion of students who do not even score "below basic." But it also needs to include attention to top-level performances, since the proportion of our students scoring in the top levels on international assessments is not as high as that in top-performing nations, and we know that many bright students are bored in high school. Rather than acrimoniously blaming teachers or parents, leaders at state and district levels need to bring together a broad range of stakeholders, including business leaders, students, parents, and educators to define both a vision of what an educated American should look like in 2030 and the steps necessary to achieve that vision.

## Ambitious Standards

Countries that excel in education set ambitious standards for their students, typically at either the national or state/provincial level. Research has shown that the standards of high-performing countries are similar and that they differ from most American state standards in several ways. According to research by Bill Schmidt, world-class content standards have greater focus than U.S. state standards; they cover a smaller number of topics in greater depth, enabling students to learn something well before they move to more difficult content. By contrast, U.S. state standards cover a large number of topics in each grade level, resulting in a curriculum that is famously "a mile wide and an inch deep." World-class standards also have greater rigor. The math and science curriculum studied by a typical American 8th grader is two years behind the curriculum being studied in the highest-performing countries. Finally, math and science standards in high-performing countries have greater coherence. Topics follow the logic of the discipline, as compared to the arbitrary "laundry list" of topics found in most U.S. standards documents, which revisit many topics too frequently across grades (NGA et al., 2008).

It is important that high standards be universal and transparent so that everyone understands what students are expected to achieve.

One reason U.S. performance is low relative to other countries is that standards and expectations vary wildly across the country, with some states and local districts setting high expectations for their students and others holding much lower standards. This analysis from international research about the need for high universal standards is leading to major changes in a number of countries. In Germany, where standards have historically been set at the state ("land") level, the states have come together to create common standards that are national but not federally controlled. Australia, another federal system, is developing not just national standards but a national curriculum, with states and the federal government working together. This remarkable development reflects an understanding that in a globalized age, the differences between states are less important than the fact that no student should have an education that is less than that provided by other states or other countries. On the other hand, in Canada, another high-performing country, the federal government has no role in education, so the standards are set at the province level (although information about each province's standards are shared through the nation's Council of Ministers). Despite the U.S. tradition of local control, it seems that local setting of standards, while perhaps appropriate for an earlier era, leads to unequal opportunity and low achievement compared with either state or national standards. Once standards are in place, it is critical that they not sit on a shelf but be clearly communicated to educators, parents, and students alike.

In the United States, the growing understanding of the importance of more rigorous and focused standards has been taken up by the Common Core State Standards movement, which is discussed in more detail in Chapter 5. In the highest-performing countries, standards are set across the whole curriculum. In contrast, the United States' tactical strategy is to focus on reading and math only, with the promise that standards for other subjects might come later. The danger in this approach is that it will further narrow the curriculum, as No Child Left Behind legislation already has by deemphasizing subjects that are not linked to standards and high-stakes assessments. Common standards are a good start, but they are only the beginning.

Standards are not self-implementing. Most, though not all, countries and provinces develop curricula to go with their standards to ensure greater consistency of implementation and teacher training and professional development that take these standards and curricula into account. External examinations focused on these curricula, often at the conclusion of lower or upper secondary school, or at the end of both (see Chapter 5), create strong incentives for teachers and students to work toward meeting the standards. Although the 1980s and 1990s saw an attempt in the United States to set standards for certain subjects, the standards were too broad and unfocused, and there was not enough effort in curriculum development, teacher training, or professional development to make these standards a reality in classrooms.

## Commitment to Equity

The long-term costs of educational failure are high for both individuals and societies. An equitable and inclusive educational system is one of the most powerful tools that a society has for increasing social equality. Leaders in most countries proclaim their commitment to equity in education, but successful education systems focus on achieving equity in a strong and deliberate way. The United States performs very poorly on international assessments compared with other countries in large part because it has such a large proportion of students scoring in the bottom quarter of the performance distribution. In every country, children of wealthier and better-educated parents do better in school than children from poorer or less-educated parents, but high-performing systems use a number of approaches to reduce the impact of social background on student achievement, creating a society that is open to talent from wherever it may come.

At the classroom level, there are a wide range of interventions that have been shown to increase academic achievement for low-income students, especially in the area of reading, the best-researched curricular area. Ontario raised the percentage of students reaching 6th grade standards in reading significantly by applying these strategies to every school in the province, rather than just a few pilot schools, as so often happens elsewhere (Levin, 2008). Finland has an early and systematic approach to intervention. Every teacher is trained to differentiate instruction for students with different skill levels. In addition, every school has a special education teacher and student support team to help the classroom teacher and catch any student who is struggling before he or she can fall too far behind. As discussed in Chapter 2, this approach to ensuring that all students reach high standards is a major reason why there is so little gap between the top- and bottom-performing students in Finland, despite a locally managed school system with only a light national hand (Sahlberg, 2011). Singapore, which has a multiethnic and multilingual population, uses structured small learning groups that meet daily for all children who require additional support in learning to read or do mathematics, starting in 1st grade. The curriculum includes English language development because, although English is the language of instruction in Singapore, there are many students who do not speak English at home.

Reforms of school structure can also enhance equity. Early tracking in elementary and lower secondary schools, for example, create greater inequity. Finland and most other European school systems have moved away from their traditionally separate academic and vocational schools at the lower secondary level, recognizing that the practice primarily reproduces the existing socioeconomic structure. When Poland abolished its separate general and vocational secondary schools in the 1990s after the end of Communist rule, it saw significant increases in its students' achievement on international assessments between 2000 and 2003, especially among lower-performing students. The United States has long had a common high school, but American high schools often have strong internal tracking systems with low-quality education in the less academic tracks and little mobility between the tracks (Oakes, 2005).

Out-of-school supports are also essential to increasing equity. Research all over the world has clearly shown the importance of cognitive and emotional development in the preschool years and the benefits of high-quality early childhood education for later success in schools (Hamburg, 1992). Most countries are therefore expanding early childhood services, either universally or for lower-income families (Kagan & Stewart, 2005).

Family structure and family engagement with education are also important. The United States has a relatively high proportion of single-parent families, and children from single-parent families score lower on average than those from two-parent families. One benefit that most Asian education systems have is a more stable family structure than exists in many Western countries; typically, two parents, and sometimes grandparents as well, are focused on a child's education. But as urbanization and modernization change societies, this family structure cannot be taken for granted. In Singapore, for example, schools work with community organizations from the three major ethnic groups to create family-like supports for areas where there are poorer or single-parent families. In the United States, community schools and Promise Neighborhoods provide such supports in some districts.

Finally, resources are necessary for providing equitable educational opportunities. Although high education expenditures don't necessarily lead to high performance—and, in fact, many of the high-performing countries have relatively modest expenditures—resources do matter. Most of the countries have relatively equal expenditures across schools. Many also have policies that permit less income inequality than in the United States and have a range of universal health and social safety net systems for families. From a research point of view, it is hard to parcel out the effects of these policies on educational achievement, but the job of school is undoubtedly more challenging when health and social supports are lacking.

Heroic teachers and principals show every day that children from disadvantaged backgrounds can achieve well in school and beat the odds, and efforts to turn around low-performing schools in American cities and rural areas are proving what targeted resources and reforms can do. But to observers from other countries, highly variable academic standards and inequalities in school structure and funding, a patchy health and social support infrastructure, and large income inequalities outside school are major reasons for the large gaps in academic performance in the United States.

High-performing countries do not fund schools from local property taxes, as the United States does, a practice that leads to more advantaged students having more resources and less advantaged students having fewer resources (OECD, 2011b). Canada used to have a system similar to that of the United States, but a few years ago, province governments responded to concerns about high property taxes and began to fund schools primarily at the province level. This has enabled provinces to develop provincewide approaches to raising achievement (Tucker, 2011). Most high-performing countries also have mechanisms for targeting additional resources to disadvantaged students or geographic areas. For example, in Shanghai, the province has worked to equalize facilities for schools serving lower-income families, and each "strong" public school in Shanghai is paired with a weaker school to strengthen leadership and teacher professional development with the goal of raising that school's achievement.

## High-Quality Teachers and Leaders

Vision and societal leadership, ambitious standards, and commitment to equity are crucial starting points, but unless they affect teaching and learning in the classroom, they will not bring about significant change. This is the heart of school improvement and the most difficult part to change.

When countries are first creating school systems, they are focused primarily on the transmission of fairly basic skills and are less concerned with the quality of the teaching force than with just getting enough teachers into schools. However, as countries seek success in the global knowledge economy, the roles set for teachers and the demands placed on them change rapidly. These countries need teachers who can prepare students with the kinds of higher-order thinking skills that knowledge workers require; help every child succeed, not just the easy-to-teach; work effectively with an ethnically diverse student population; and harness new technologies. There seems to be a broad consensus that no matter what reform strategy is being pursued, the overall quality of a school system rests on the quality of its teachers, and the quality of teachers depends on the system in place to support them. In modern diversified economies, teaching has to compete with other sectors for talent. Therefore, successful countries are placing great emphasis on the recruitment, preparation, support, distribution, compensation, and evaluation of teachers—the front lines in education (Asia Society, 2011).

But the effective deployment of high-quality teachers requires capable people up the line, as well. As higher-performing systems devolve more responsibility to the school level, they are rethinking the recruitment, training, and role of school principals. Schools cannot be turned around or driven to higher achievement without strong and effective leadership focused on results. The different strategies that countries like Australia, Canada, Singapore, England, and Finland are pursuing to elevate the teaching profession and develop effective leadership are described in more detail in Chapter 4.

Beyond the school level, leadership in city, state, or national departments of education must be strong as well. In Singapore, the high levels of expertise in the Ministry of Education are a critical ingredient in the focused design, careful implementation, and nuanced assessment of successful education quality improvements. Educated at some of the world's best universities and deeply experienced in school practice, leaders at the ministry demonstrate knowledge of education policy and practice that is second to none. In Canada, Ontario's Literacy and Numeracy Initiatives were driven by expert capacity in a new unit within the provincial Ministry of Education, as well as by the development of literacy and numeracy teams and specialized student success personnel in districts. In contrast, the United States has been losing expertise in state education departments, in district offices, and within the U.S. Department of Education for many years. The functions of most staff in these organizations have become focused more on monitoring compliance with program regulations than on providing expertise and helping schools implement significant improvement efforts.

## Alignment and Coherence

One of the big differences between the United States and high-performing countries is the United States' lack of alignment between the goals of the education system (expressed at the national, state, or district level) and actual practice in schools and classrooms. High-performing countries demonstrate that there are various ways to produce alignment and coherence.

Singapore, for example, has a "tightly coupled" system in which the Ministry of Education, the teacher training center known as the National Institute of Education (NIE), cluster superintendents, principals, and master teachers all work closely together to bring about any change in practice. Finland's very different system has lots of local autonomy but ensures consistency of teaching approaches and practice through government-funded university teacher preparation programs, all of which share a common philosophy and approach to education; high-quality teachers; and networking among schools to share best practices. Many high-performing countries have coherent instruction and examinations systems in which the standards are developed into curricula and syllabus-based examinations and also serve as the basis for teacher preparation and professional development (Fuchs & Woessman, 2004). In East Asian systems, teachers work together every week to improve lessons and routinely open their classrooms to other teachers. These practices produce consistent instruction and a way to disseminate new curricula that produces consistent practice across large numbers of schools.

The United States, in contrast, is a "loosely coupled" system—so loosely coupled that it is almost incoherent. By the time a reform from the federal government reaches the schools, it may be unrecognizable. Too often, schools lack the systematic supports they need to enact these reforms, meaning there is a large "implementation gap" between policies and the classroom (Fullan, 2001). And the elements of the system are not aligned. At one level, U.S. educators might establish an ambitious goal like teaching higher-order thinking skills but then go on to measure student achievement with tests that assess only basic skills. A further problem is the lack of alignment between K–12 education and university-based teacher preparation institutions, where the curriculum is determined by faculty who often have little regular interaction with schools. In recent years, the United States has been trying to address this lack of alignment through the use of test-based accountability in reading and math, such as that addressed by the No Child Left Behind legislation. While this practice has improved alignment, it has produced another set of problems through the side effects of narrowing the curriculum, use of inappropriate tests, and so on. High-performing systems take pains to ensure that all of the elements—standards, curriculum, teacher preparation, assessment, and professional development—contribute to the goal of raising standards and closing achievement gaps.

## Management and Accountability

All education systems struggle with the balance between centralization and decentralization, between top-down prescription and bottom-up responsibility. In recent years, more traditionally centralized systems, like China and Singapore, have been devolving more responsibility to the school level while other systems, like England under Tony Blair's government, Australia, and the United States through federal legislation, have been asserting more central control in order to try to drive performance and create more accountability.

Getting accountability right is crucial, and there are many different forms of it to consider. Managerial accountability is similar to that found in companies, where an upper level of management requires evidence of performance and obtains that evidence from inspection systems or output scores. The No Child Left Behind legislation focuses on this kind of managerial, test-based accountability. While this kind of accountability has brought attention to groups that had previously been neglected, it has also led to the distortion, downgrading, and narrowing of the curriculum and has not done much to develop lower-performing schools' capacity to progress toward high achievement. At the other extreme, in Finland, the highest performer in Europe, there is no external inspection of schools or external testing until the secondary school leaving exam. Instead, accountability rests on the trust placed by families and government in the high quality and professional skill of the teachers. Singapore has a system in which multiple types of accountability come into play. The performance management system for teachers and principals centers on the setting of annual goals and their assessment by a wide range of professionals and on a wide range of indicators, including student performance as well as contributions to school and community, relationship with parents, and successful completion of professional development, but it also invests considerable resources in building capacity in schools through attracting and retaining high-quality teachers and allowing them to exercise professional judgment.

Change processes invariably need a mixture of carrots and sticks. Overreliance on simple, test-based accountability does not move schools to high standards. "You cannot bludgeon people into greatness," says Ben Levin, former Deputy Minister of Education in Ontario (Asia Society, 2011, p. 13). However, uninformed professional judgment is no more effective. What systems that are high performing or significantly improving do is combine intelligent, multifaceted, transparent accountability with initiatives that build professional knowledge and capacity to implement and evaluate best practices at the school level. Doing so creates a culture of continuous improvement and ever-higher expectations.

## Student Motivation

Anyone who has ever visited classrooms in Singapore or China cannot help but be impressed by the intense engagement of students with the lesson and by the sheer amount of time students study outside school. Dating, television, and sports all take a backseat to schoolwork. An intense belief in meritocracy—the idea that effort, not ability, is the prime determinant of success—combined with an examination system that creates a strong incentive to work hard and the value placed on education by families as a route to social mobility in societies where there is or has recently been real poverty all create a powerful motivation to study hard.

In Finnish classrooms, students are also intently engaged, albeit through different means. Finnish education is rooted in ideas of discovery and self-directed learning. Students work on their own or in groups on problems and projects, often of their own design, from elementary school on. In addition, each school has a range of mechanisms, including special teachers and pupils' care groups, designed to ensure that every individual student feels able to succeed academically.

However, every country has students with varying degrees of motivation. An educational leader in Shanghai told me he had two kinds of parents: "the overbearing and the uninvolved." It is the schools' job to engage and support students even when they may not initially be motivated to succeed. In Singapore, for example, the government supports community groups to help children and families who are not successfully engaged in school, and the evaluations of all Singaporean teachers address their work with and relationships to the parents of the students in their charge. Multiple paths to success and schools with many different themes have been created to engage all students. For example, a strong and well-funded vocational education system keeps less academically inclined students engaged with school, enabling some of them to later go on to university. In Ontario, a new data system enables the school to identify students at risk of dropping out, and schools assign student success officers to work individually with each student to help them find a path to graduation. The province also developed new "high-skills" majors. Countries that are successful with all students are designing multiple pathways to graduation and to achieving high standards.

Why is it so hard to motivate all students? After reviewing the research on student motivation, Goslin (2003) argues that there are four things we need to do to increase student motivation and engagement: (1) modify our belief in the importance of effort versus ability; (2) increase the distribution of rewards for academic achievement so that so that they go to more than just the top students; (3) ensure that teachers have access to the best classroom practices on instruction and engagement; and (4) rebalance the time devoted to competing demands like television, social activities, or employment after school versus studying. High-performing countries employ both intrinsic and extrinsic incentives for students and expect more time on task than is typical in many American schools.

## Global and Future Orientation

Recognizing the kind of interconnected world into which we are moving, high-performing countries are trying to develop a global orientation among their teachers, school leaders, and students in their teaching, curriculum, and international school partnerships and exchanges. Countries that have high-achieving educational systems have all also used international benchmarking studies as a way to improve their systems to move up the educational value chain. How do countries learn? The education departments in some countries have specialists whose job it is to understand and follow developments in other countries and assess the potential of those developments for local application. Others send teams around the world to study some high-performing countries or to analyze different approaches and experiences with a specific education question that confronts them. China, for example, sent teams to 30 countries to study their curricula before introducing their curriculum modernization effort. The Ontario premier visited England to examine the workings of their literacy and numeracy strategies, and afterward, the Ontario Ministry of Education took the limitations of the English experience into account when designing Ontario's approach to literacy and numeracy education. Singapore has looked at assessment systems in Australia, Hong Kong, Scotland, and Australia. All of the countries in this book have been very active in conducting these types of exercises. Some countries have brought in experts from other countries to act as a kind of "visiting committee" to provide input to proposed reforms or have hired short- or long-term advisors when redesigning some aspect of their systems.

Until recently, American education leaders have not been very active in seeking out innovations and successful experiences in other countries, but this is starting to change. North Carolina is one state that has studied education systems internationally as a way to inspire and drive its own education reforms, taking delegations of district superintendents, members of the state board of education and legislature, and state business leaders to visit countries that have a close relationship with North Carolina or use best practices relevant to its system. Mayor Bloomberg held a global cities conference in New York City in 2010 to share best practices and implementation challenges faced by the world's largest cities. Most prominently, Secretary of Education Arne Duncan, together with the National Education Association (NEA), American Federation of Teachers (AFT), OECD, Education International (EI), Council of Chief State School Officers (CCSSO), Asia Society, and the New York public television station WNET, held the International Summit on the Teaching Profession in March 2011, reflections on which appear in Chapter 4.

Finally, high-performing countries are oriented more toward the future than the past. Singapore, for example, regularly conducts visioning exercises, scanning the global horizon in order to create "future school designs," and Alberta engaged in a provincewide public dialogue as to what an educated Albertan in 2039 should look like as a backdrop for revised education goals and legislative initiatives.

There is no one way to run an effective national or state system of education. All systems must struggle with finding the right balance between top-down and bottom-up, between uniformity and diversity, between central control and local autonomy. In general, when achievement is low and uneven, strong government intervention is needed. But moving a system from good to great—making every school a great school—entails going beyond top-down, prescriptive interventions that have dominated many reforms and narrowed the curriculum to a small range of subjects and lower-order skills. It means focusing on building the capacity of schools and generating a professional knowledge culture in which best practice is codified and shared. It is essential to design polices and structures that address performance deficits among low-income and minority children while providing for all children the higher-order thinking skills and broader curriculum needed in a global, knowledge-based economy. Success requires a clear vision and sense of moral purpose, a guiding and persistent political coalition, ambitious standards and a commitment to quality, effective leadership at every level, a focus on building teacher capacity to make the needed improvements, engagement of students, and broader community support.

 ## Reflection Questions

As you consider the ways in which Singapore, the Canadian provinces of Alberta and Ontario, Shanghai, Australia, and Finland have each raised their student achievement to the top of the world and the key elements they all share, here are some questions to stimulate a discussion of how your state or district could meet world-class standards. How does your state or district stack up on these elements of high-performing systems?

1. *Vision and leadership:* What is your state's or district's vision for what an educated American should look like in 2030? Can you engage your students, parents, teachers, and business leaders and community organizations in reaching consensus on what knowledge and skills will be essential and form an ongoing leadership coalition to take and monitor strategic steps toward that new vision?

2. *Ambitious standards:* High-performing countries have ambitious standards across the curriculum that are understood by students, parents, and teachers alike. To start, can you construct an implementation plan for the curriculum, instructional, and professional development supports that would be needed to get all students to achieve the Common Core standards in reading and math? (See Chapter 5.)

3. *Commitment to equity:* How well would your lowest-performing students do on the PISA science assessment? (Sample questions are available from the OECD PISA website at www.oecd.org/data-oecd/47/23/41943106.pdf.) What would it take in terms of classroom interventions, changes in school structure, multiple pathways, out-of-school supports, professional development, and targeted resources for low-performing schools to set a high floor of achievement in your state or district?

4. *High-quality teachers and leaders:* What steps can your state or district take to raise the quality of teaching and leadership to match the new challenges? (See Chapter 4 for a detailed discussion of how

high-performing countries recruit, prepare, support, reward, and retain high-quality teachers and leaders.)

5. *Alignment and coherence:* High-performing countries perform well because all parts of the system work together toward achieving their standards. In the United States, there is typically an "implementation gap" between a state's or district's goals and what happens in classrooms. What are the causes of the implementation gap and the barriers to change in your jurisdiction? What bold action could you take to eliminate those causes?

6. *Management and accountability:* Taking the vision and standards you have laid out as your school system's five-year goals, what kinds of teachers and knowledge sharing will your system need in order to develop the professional capacity necessary to meet those goals? What should be the goal for Year 1? Year 2? How would you measure progress toward those goals in a fair and transparent way?

7. *Student engagement and motivation:* How motivated are your students to study and learn? Can you identify those students who are bored or disengaged, whether because the work is not challenging enough or because they are falling behind and, as in Ontario, create a student success plan for each of them?

8. *Global and future orientation:* The world is changing fast, and schools cannot stand still. Review what other countries do to keep abreast of the world's evolving educational standards and best practices, and discuss ideas of how to impart a more global perspective in your school. (See Chapter 6 for ideas.)

# 4

# DEVELOPING EFFECTIVE TEACHERS AND SCHOOL LEADERS

Just as a country is as good as its people, so its citizens are only as good as their teachers. —**Lee Hsien Loong, Prime Minister of Singapore**

When people describe the teachers who had the greatest impact on them, they invariably describe ones who were caring, passionate about their subject, and good at getting them to do their very best. But how do we find such teachers? This is the central challenge facing countries across the globe as they seek to develop first-class education systems to prepare students for the fast-changing global knowledge economy of the 21st century.

As nations try to increase both educational access and achievement, there are great debates about how to get the policy infrastructure right. But even the best policies cannot succeed without qualified, dedicated, skilled personnel in place to implement those policies, so the issues of teacher quality and, more recently, principal quality are becoming central to the educational agenda of every country.

The challenge is becoming even more acute as the roles of teachers change. Countries in the early stages of educational development, focused on expanding access to elementary and lower secondary education and providing for transmission of fairly basic skills, are less concerned with the quality of the teaching force than with getting enough teachers into classrooms. But as countries enter the global knowledge economy and seek to prepare their students for an innovation-oriented, science- and technology-driven economy, they need teachers who can prepare students with the kinds of higher-order cognitive skills they need to become knowledge workers, not just factory workers; who can help every child succeed, not just those who are easy to teach; who can address the increasing ethnic diversity of many school systems; and who can adapt to and harness new technologies. The stakes could not be higher for individuals and for education systems. Recognizing that teachers are the single biggest in-school influence on student achievement, there seems to be a global consensus that no matter what reform strategy is being pursued, "the quality of a school system cannot exceed the quality of its teachers" (Barber & Mourshed, 2007).

Contrary to conventional wisdom, a high-quality teacher workforce is not due simply to a traditional cultural respect for the teaching profession; it comes as a result of deliberate policy choices pursued over a number of years. High-performing countries build their human resource systems by investing energy up front to attract, prepare, and support good teachers, rather than using energy on the back end to reduce teacher attrition and fire weak teachers (Stewart, 2011a). They also systemically identify and nurture leadership talent to manage schools with the goal of increasing student achievement. There is much innovation around the world on these issues, as was shown during the International Summit on the Teaching Profession, held in New York City in March 2011 and attended by ministers of education, heads of teachers' unions, and other teacher leaders from 16 nations (Asia Society, 2011).

Around the world, systems that excel in education do so thanks to a wide array of purposeful strategies. This chapter presents some examples of how high-performing and rapidly improving nations are building their teaching workforce. As you read, think about how some of these ideas might be adapted to help develop more effective educators in your district or state.

## Attracting and Recruiting Teachers

Many countries have deep concerns about a number of issues related to teacher training and retention: widespread teacher shortages, especially in certain subjects or geographic areas due to large-scale retirement; high and costly attrition of teachers; the declining attractiveness and status of the profession as other career opportunities open up for women and minorities; and a political and media climate that blames teachers or their unions for all the ills of schools.

Some countries respond by lowering standards for entry into teaching, but high-performing countries pay significant attention to attracting and carefully selecting high-quality workers for the teaching profession. For example, when Finland raised the standards required to become a teacher in 1979, they found that as they increased the status of teachers, they actually attracted more applicants. At that time, all teacher preparation was moved to the university level, and eventually research-based master's degrees were required of all licensed teachers. As the government became more confident in the quality and training of teachers, they gradually devolved more and more responsibility to them for the development of curricula, assessment, and the overall quality of schools. Teaching is now a highly sought career in Finland, where only 1 in 10 applicants is accepted into the wholly government-funded teacher preparation programs after two rounds of selection. The most able young people in Finland see teaching as an independent and respected profession with considerable autonomy, comparable to doctors or architects, rather than a job that involves mere technical implementation of externally mandated standards and tests (Sahlberg, 2011).

Other countries don't just wait for prospective teachers to apply; they actively recruit them. Singapore has a systemwide recruitment process under which the Ministry of Education selects prospective teachers from the top one-third of their cohort for four-year undergraduate teacher preparation programs or, if they enter later, a one-year graduate program. Principals sit on the recruitment interview panels. Candidates are required to have strong academic records and evidence a deep commitment to the profession and to serving the diverse students of

Singapore. Those selected as trainee teachers are put on the ministry payroll and receive a stipend while in training, and they commit to teaching for a minimum of three years (Ho, personal interview, August 2010). Singapore also actively recruits mid career candidates, believing that their experience in the world of work is valuable to students. For example, when Singapore expanded its arts programs in schools and thus needed more art teachers, the ministry set up recruitment stations at major museum art exhibits and other places that attract artists.

In China, the massive and rapid expansion of education and the overall economy over the past 20 years created major teacher shortages, especially in rural areas, where poorly qualified teachers taught in village schools. China's education policymakers are now paying significant attention to recruiting, training, and improving the quality of the nation's 12 million teachers. Salaries have been raised to be equivalent to those for civil service, and the central government contributes part of the cost of salaries in poorer regions to help attract more applicants. Scholarships for teacher training are offered to young people who live in rural areas in order to develop a supply of teachers for those regions (Asia Society, 2006b). In cities, higher education institutions that train teachers give early admission to student teacher candidates so that they can attract better students.

In England, teaching had become an unattractive occupation for college graduates in the 1990s, and there were persistent shortages in a number of fields. Starting in 2000, the government of Prime Minister Tony Blair took a series of steps to raise the status of the teaching profession and recruit more and higher-quality teachers. Some changes were made in compensation and working conditions, but a sophisticated advertising campaign using modern marketing techniques was a major contributor to the turnaround strategy that within five years resulted in eight teacher applications for every open position (Day, 2011).

In modern, diversified economies, education has to compete with other sectors for talent. High-performing education systems overcome the challenges of attracting high-quality people into teaching and grant the profession higher status using intelligent incentives that are applied over a period of time. When shortages occur, the focus is on enacting

## "Making a Difference":
## Tackling Teacher Shortages in England

The sophisticated national advertising campaign the British government developed to attract citizens to the teaching profession divided potential teachers into three groups—those planning on teaching, those considering teaching, and those who had not considered teaching—and tried to understand each group's motivations and barriers to entering teacher training. For those planning on teaching, the main motivators were the social value of the profession, working with children, and love of the subject, but for those not planning to teach—especially in shortage fields like math and science—financial incentives were more important. The government mounted a multiyear advertising campaign with the theme "Making a Difference" to raise the status of the profession and combined that with financial incentives for teacher training as well as hiring bonuses that were larger for individuals teaching subject areas that were hard to staff. A telephone line encouraged people to call for more information, and each call was followed up with information on how to become a teacher and the subsidies available. A program called Teach First, similar to Teach for America, offering two-year contracts to teach in poor-performing schools, was used to attract very bright graduates into the profession, but a larger emphasis was put on recruiting people over the age of 25 who were interested in changing careers. For these groups, a wide range of alternate routes into teaching were created that allowed them to qualify as a teacher while they worked in a school. These teachers also received a training subsidy that helped to offset the salary cuts that many faced as they switched careers. (About half of all teacher training recruits are now over the age of 25.) The Training and Development Agency of the Department of Education in England, the agency responsible for all these measures, also offered six-month courses to people with

*continued*

**"Making a Difference":**
**Tackling Teacher Shortages in England** (*continued*)

quantitative backgrounds to enable them to become math, chemistry, and physics teachers. During the financial crisis of the late 2000s, a "bankers to teachers" campaign was developed, and a new effort to attract the top academic graduates into teaching has also begun. The result of all of these measures has been a notable increase in the number of calls to the government's teacher recruitment telephone line, a substantial reduction and even erasure of teacher deficits in shortage subject areas like math and science, and the rise of teaching from 92nd on a list of career choices to a top career choice within five years.

better recruitment policies rather than lowering standards to get more teachers. Because they recognize that teaching for understanding and problem solving and holding all learners to high standards require a deeper knowledge of subject matter, the emphasis is on raising the bar for those going into teaching. Singapore and Finland both draw their teachers from the top one-third of an education cohort. Other countries think that since teaching is such a large profession, it is not realistic to focus only on academic high fliers. Qualities such as passion and commitment to students may be equally if not more important. Nevertheless, all high-performing countries make attracting talented people to the profession a central part of their education policies and practices.

More fundamentally, a more professional environment in schools is necessary to attract high-caliber recruits. Attracting top talent requires attention to the whole system: the quality of teacher preparation, a professional work environment, and attractive career opportunities.

## Preparing 21st Century Teachers

Most countries do not limit entry into teacher preparation programs. A problem with this approach is that it can lead to an oversupply of teacher candidates. Course enrollments may then be larger than they need to be, and graduating teachers may have difficulty finding jobs. This, in turn, gives the profession lower status, and the quality of workers going into the profession tends to decline. High-performing countries tend to have more selective enrollment in teacher education programs, either through directly managing the recruitment and selection process or setting the standards for selection, or through limiting the number of places in teacher education programs. This approach makes the profession more attractive to highly talented candidates, and better job placement rates further increase the status of the profession.

Whatever the selection mechanism, there is a universal concern that colleges of education are not responding quickly enough to rapid global changes and changes in educational needs. Teacher education is regarded as too theoretical, and universities are criticized for not taking responsibility for the quality of their teacher graduates. Countries are taking different approaches to modernizing teacher education. In China, Finland, and Singapore, for example, traditional teacher preparation programs are accepted and valued, and adaptations to changing skill needs are made within the existing institutional framework. England, on the other hand, chose to create alternate routes to teacher certification to compete with traditional providers. Graduates of traditional and alternate certification routes have to meet the same criteria. As more countries look to recruit high-quality, midcareer workers into teaching, adaptations of traditional teacher preparation programs will likely become more common.

Two countries with well-regarded teacher preparation programs are Finland and Singapore. In Finland, all teachers except preschool teachers must hold a two-year master's degree, which follows an undergraduate degree in one or more subjects. Finland prides itself on research-based teacher education. The curriculum covers educational theory and research methodology, and students learn how to design and conduct original research in classrooms. It is also strong on practical training. A supervised practicum in a model school associated with a university accounts for 15 to 25 percent of teachers' overall preparation time. In these schools, supervising teachers are specially selected and trained to ensure that they can model effective practice and coach new teachers. There is also extensive preparation on student assessment, differentiated instruction for special needs students, curriculum development, and pedagogical content knowledge, including cooperative and problem-based learning, since these are all skills that teachers will need in Finnish schools. The high quality of Finnish schools depends on the excellence of their entering teachers (Sahlberg, 2011).

In Singapore, all teachers are trained at the National Institute of Education (NIE), a part of Nanyang Technological University. NIE has a strong base of subject matter and pedagogical content knowledge experts and close ties to schools. Singapore's teachers are generally considered well trained. Nevertheless, in 2009, in response to the rapid pace of global change taking place, NIE conducted a review of their teacher preparation program and developed a new Teacher Education Model for the 21st Century (TE21). The theme of the model is that 21st century learners need 21st century teachers, who not only possess 21st century literacies themselves but also can create the learning environments that enable their students to develop such skills (NIE, 2009). Many of the changes being made under TE21 echo the reforms being made in teacher education in a number of countries:

• There are clear standards for what graduates should know and be able to do in each subject area.

• Teacher preparation programs are willing to be held accountable for initial teacher competencies.

• There is more emphasis on guided practice in classroom settings from the very beginning.

• Teacher education institutions are more involved in mentoring beginning teachers in schools.

• Teacher candidates develop a wider pedagogical repertoire, including cooperative and inquiry-based learning.

• Teacher candidates develop greater capacity to incorporate Internet and communication technology (ICT) into their instruction.

• Teachers develop greater facility in using data and assessment to guide instruction.

• Service learning is required to promote understanding of communities.

• Teacher candidates learn research skills so that they can diagnose and solve problems based on evidence.

## Professional Development

According to Malcolm Gladwell (2008), it takes professionals roughly 10,000 hours before they feel expert at their job. Today, as the requirements of teaching constantly evolve and subject matter is continually updated, even the best preservice teacher preparation program can't prepare teachers for all the changes and challenges they will encounter throughout their career. Therefore, a continuum of regular professional development from beginning teaching (induction) to advanced practice is essential to effective teaching and learning. International surveys reveal wide variation in how much professional development teachers receive. Too many new teachers in the United States are left to sink or swim without significant mentoring or assistance, leaving them feeling ineffective and unsupported. It is no wonder that one-third of American teachers leave within their first five years in the profession, an attrition rate that costs school districts billions of dollars (Darling-Hammond & Rothman, 2011). For those teachers who do receive professional development, there is a preponderance of ineffective, one-off seminars, so-called "drive-by" professional development, rather than the kind of long-term support with feedback and opportunity for practice that is thought to be more effective and connected to school improvement. Policy reforms at the district, state, or national level are often enacted, one after the other, without the teacher training to build the capacity to carry them out, undermining the reforms and leading invariably to implementation gaps.

In high-performing and improving countries, all beginning teachers receive mentoring assistance for a year or two, and all teachers have time to observe other teachers' classrooms and participate in organized professional development that is tied to either school improvement or career development or both. For example, in 2004, Ontario moved from a system of teacher testing that had been considered punitive by the profession and had not encouraged teachers to be meaningfully engaged in their own learning to a system focused on teacher development. One aspect of the new system is that every beginning teacher participates in a supervised induction program that includes support and feedback. This has sharply reduced attrition among new teachers and also provides annual feedback to policymakers on specific teaching needs (Levin, 2008). In another Canadian province, Alberta, the Alberta Initiative for School Improvement (AISI) has introduced and supported school-based, teacher-led study initiatives focused on enhancing student engagement and improving student performance. This action research is additionally intended to improve teachers' skill using data and research findings in instructional decision making (AISI, n.d.).

East Asian countries such as Japan, Korea, and China employ what is essentially an apprenticeship framework in which there is a systematic effort to pass on the accumulated wisdom of teaching practice in particular fields. In Japan, all teachers participate regularly in lesson study, a practice in which groups of teachers review their lesson plans and determine how to improve them, in part through analysis of student errors. For example, observers of Japanese elementary classrooms have long noted the consistent quality and thoroughness of math lessons. Teachers have learned through their lesson study groups how to introduce a mathematical concept, use skillful questioning to elicit a discussion of mathematical ideas, including incorrect ones, and review the key concept again at the end. Lesson study is a mechanism for teacher self-reflection as well as a tool for continuous improvement (Stevenson & Stigler, 2006).

The practice of school-by-school lesson study often culminates in large public research lessons. For example, when the topic of solar cells was added to Japan's elementary science curriculum, the national guidelines furnished only learning objectives, not teaching methods. Lesson study groups of teachers and researchers across the country reviewed research and curriculum materials and tried out their ideas in classrooms. After about a year of progressive refinement, thousands of teachers, researchers, and policymakers participated, many via video, in a series of public research lessons, observing and asking questions about particular approaches. Through these means, information about effective ways to teach about solar cells spread widely among schools and influenced the ways in which textbooks treated the subject.

In China, classrooms are routinely open for observation by other teachers, teacher trainees, and administrators, and teachers are required to observe and provide feedback on a certain number of colleagues' lessons each year. This openness of Chinese classrooms is in strong contrast to the informal "closed-door" classrooms in the United States and can be viewed as a form of both public and professional accountability. Chinese teachers also take part in weekly subject-based teacher study groups that focus on curriculum, lesson planning, and classroom improvement. The groups, led by senior teachers, exist in every school and are connected to the district education department, which in turn is connected to the provincial education department, which works closely with the Basic Education Department of the Ministry of Education. Thus, with any change in curriculum, there is an immediate way to get new materials, publications, videos to teachers and into classrooms. There is also a national television channel devoted to teacher development. Therefore, even though China's rapid educational expansion has meant a persistent shortage of qualified teachers, especially in rural areas, there is an ongoing, organized, nationwide (but decentralized) system of professional development in place to upgrade the quality of teaching (Asia Society & CCSSO, 2010).

In Singapore, 100 hours of professional development is guaranteed to each teacher every year and may be acquired in several ways. Courses at the NIE, for example, focus on subject matter and pedagogical knowledge and lead toward higher degrees. Much of professional development, however, is school based, led by staff whose job it is to know where there are problems in the school (e.g., with a group's math performance) or to introduce new practices such as project-based learning or new uses of ICT (Sclafani, 2008). In addition, each school has access to a fund intended to support teacher growth; a school might, for example, send staff to other countries to develop new perspectives by examining specific aspects of practice. Teachers also work with researchers at NIE to conduct action research in classrooms. Much of this research is focused on the efforts put forward under the "Thinking Schools, Learning Nation" and "Teach Less, Learn More" policy directions to broaden the range of pedagogical approaches used in Singapore classrooms. Teacher networks and learning circles encourage peer-to-peer learning, and a new Academy of Singapore Teachers opened in 2010. "The goal is to have the teaching profession take more responsibility for continuous improvement of practice," said Manogaran Suppiah, director of the academy. Master teachers in different subject areas and different schools will develop courses to spread best practices across schools. In order to make time for teachers to engage in deep improvement of their practice, teachers teach classes for approximately 20 to 25 hours a week and have about 20 hours per week for preparing lessons, observing in other classrooms, working with students outside the classroom, or engaging in professional development.

Richard Elmore, a professor of Educational Leadership at Harvard University, famously said that teaching is a profession without a practice. But in some Asian countries, a consistent professional practice is being developed. It is continuous—recognition that best practices need to constantly evolve—and based on the premise that knowledge of good instruction is spread by teachers watching one another teach and collaborating to improve their instruction. American teachers put great stress on autonomy and independence; they close their classroom doors. The trade-off tends to be isolation, a lack of collaboration, and little peer learning. East Asian concepts of professionalism put greater emphasis on learning from professional colleagues and working in school teams to improve instruction (Stewart, 2011a).

How do high-performing countries find the time and resources for such extensive, continuous development? In Asia, there is generally a trade-off between larger class sizes—either all or some of the time—and time for professional development. "Do you use the marginal additional teacher to bring down class size or to improve the professional quality of the school, and do you have enough high-quality teachers to bring down class size?" asked S Iswaran, then Singapore's senior minister of state for education, at the March 2011 International Summit on the Teaching Profession. In Finland, students spend fewer hours in school and, while there, work more on independent projects, thus allowing teachers more time for professional responsibilities other than direct classroom teaching, such as providing individual feedback to students, meeting with families, or collaboratively diagnosing classroom problems and designing solutions.

High-performing systems have a systematic approach to professional development, focusing on more effective forms and linking them closely to both the instructional goals of the school and career opportunities for teachers.

## Evaluation and Compensation

It is an understatement to say that, all over the world, educators are in search of an effective way to evaluate and improve the work of teachers and that there is, as yet, no international consensus based on experience or research as to the best ways to do it. International surveys of teachers show that they do welcome feedback as a way to enhance their teaching (OECD, 2011a). However, they are skeptical if evaluation is performed in an unfair way or by principals who have neither the time nor the expertise to judge effective practice, or when outstanding performance does not lead to any recognition or career advancement. Overall, there is a trend toward devising appraisal systems that can drive improvement of professional practice and student achievement and away from an earlier focus on monitoring compliance with policies and procedures. But the questions of what criteria to use for appraisal, how to balance the improvement versus accountability functions, how to connect improved practice to career advancement, and whether the quality of practice should be tied to compensation are the subject of unresolved, often contentious, debates everywhere, although they take different forms in different countries.

Some countries, such as Japan and Norway, put greater weight on school evaluation than individual teacher evaluation, believing that student achievement is often the result of the efforts of many teachers rather than an individual teacher. Group evaluation, whether of whole schools or of groups of teachers, is thought to promote greater collaboration and sharing of best practices among teachers and to foster cohesion among staff.

At the March 2011 International Summit on the Teaching Profession, held in New York City, there was broad agreement that to be fair and effective in improving education on a broad scale, appraisal of individual teacher performance needs to be part of a *system* of educator development, conducted by people who have training in evaluating teaching and incorporating multiple measures to reflect the full range of teachers' work so as to avoid the distortion in behavior that comes from a narrow focus on student test scores. These principles are exemplified in Singapore's comprehensive performance management system.

In Singapore, all teachers' performance is appraised annually by several fellow professionals within the school on a broad range of measures, not just examination results. Also considered are their contribution to the academic and character development of students, their collaboration with parents and community groups, the professional development they have undertaken, their pedagogical initiatives, and their contribution to their colleagues and to the school as a whole. The system, developed in 2001 with teacher input, has been refined over time. Based on the results of this annual appraisal, teachers can receive a bonus of 10 to 30 percent of their base salary and prospects for promotion along one of three paths.

The purpose of the evaluation process in Singapore is to create a dialogue between teachers and their supervisors that is regular, frequent, clear, and intended primarily to help teachers improve and keep up with change. Every teacher sets a professional development plan for every school year, and this serves as the basis for midyear and end-of-year reviews. Teachers have access to 100 hours of professional development in support of their goals, and areas of weakness identified during evaluation process become the focus of teachers' professional development plans for the following year. The process is time-consuming but seen as worth it, as the development of teaching competency is viewed as a career-long undertaking.

Areas for improvement are also identified to form the basis of a personal professional development plan for the following year, in support of which teachers have access to 100 hours of professional development. Teachers also receive reimbursements for improving their knowledge and skills, such as language learning or technology training. This system of evaluation sits within a broader system for developing effective educators. "If you have to focus on firing an ineffective teacher, then the system has failed," said Iswaran (2011).

In most countries, entry-level salaries for teachers tend to be somewhat below those of other college graduates, although Japan, Singapore, and China attempt to peg them at or above the salaries for new civil servants. Beyond the entry level, working conditions—being treated as a professional, having the opportunity to work with colleagues, and attaining career advancement—seem more important to teachers in most countries than salary per se (Schleicher & Stewart, 2008). About half the countries in the OECD do offer some form of additional pay for outstanding performance, primarily based on the judgments of professional colleagues. Some high-performing systems like those in Finland and Canada do not support merit pay approaches, believing there is not enough empirical evidence to support their effectiveness. But in others, such as those in Shanghai and Singapore, teachers can receive significant financial bonuses and promotions based on performance evaluations.

## Teacher Distribution

In the United States, the distribution of teachers by qualifications and experience is highly unequal, with the least experienced teachers working in the schools where students have the greatest needs. This fact is a significant factor in the distribution of unequal educational outcomes.

In countries that have a uniformly strong profession, such as Finland, this issue becomes relatively unimportant, although the Finnish government does provide some salary supplements to retain teachers in rural areas. However, most larger countries do have to pay attention to teacher distribution. In China, where there has been massive migration to the cities, it is increasingly difficult to find teachers willing to work in rural areas. Consequently, China provides scholarships to people in rural areas to train as teachers. Rural teachers also earn 10 percent more through supplements from the central government and may have housing built for them. They also receive long-distance professional development through satellite television, the Internet, and the organization of schools into clusters with one central resource center for materials and assistance (Asia Society & CCSSO, 2010). The Japanese government also provides additional funds to poorer provinces so that they can attract their share of good teachers. The Australian federal government, too, gives financial incentives to teach in rural areas, away from the coasts where most young Australians prefer to live. In fact, giving bonuses to teach in hard-to-staff rural or urban schools is a common practice globally (McGaw, 2010). In addition, in some places such as Singapore and Shanghai, cities assign teachers of different levels of experience and expertise to different schools to ensure a balance of good teachers among schools.

## Career Paths and Leadership Roles

A significant barrier to retaining talented teachers in the United States is that the career structure is relatively flat. Although some districts have master teacher roles, on the whole, if teachers want to earn more money or broaden their professional practice, they have to become an administrator, where the overload of budget, disciplinary, and administrative tasks makes it difficult for them to play an instructional leadership role.

Recognizing that teachers cannot be expected to stay in the same role for 30 years, high-performing countries pay systematic attention to career development. In Singapore, there is an explicit policy of identifying and nurturing talent: after three years of teaching, teachers are assessed to see whether they have the potential for one of three different career paths—master teacher, specialist in curriculum or research, or school leader. Progress along each of these tracks is supported by additional training and annual performance reviews. Each step forward along the path comes with salary increases, and a master teacher or senior specialist can earn as much as a principal. Senior teachers play major leadership roles in schools. Surveys of Singapore teachers show that they stay in the profession because of good compensation benchmarked against market rates, positive school cultures with a strong sense of mission, and the wide range of opportunities for professional growth (Stewart, 2011b).

China has also developed well-established paths for professional advancement in teaching. There are four grades of teachers, with promotion to each one based on the demonstrated quality of lessons, support for younger teachers, and for the most senior grades, research and publications. As teachers advance, they play broader roles in curriculum design, professional development, and support for other teachers in their school, city, or province. Outstanding teachers are recognized on National Teachers' Day.

In Finland, by contrast, schools tend to be small and the career structure for teachers is relatively flat. The compensation is not extraordinarily high. Still, teachers have high levels of responsibility for curriculum planning, student progress, and assessment, and the autonomy and status they enjoy in the school and broader society make teaching a very engaging career. Teachers have relatively short teaching hours to enable them to take on these other roles. The Finnish system does not employ test-based accountability to drive its system, nor does it have a strong system of inspection of schools. Instead, the Finnish system relies on the expertise and professional accountability of teachers who are knowledgeable, academically strong, well educated, and committed to their students and communities. "We are so proud of our teachers," said Henna Virkkunen, then Finland's minister of education, at the International Summit.

In high-performing systems, teachers are able to play leadership roles and assume additional responsibility for their school's teaching and learning practices, curriculum and assessment, and technology use, all without leaving the classroom, and they improve their own skills and knowledge in the process. Increasingly, as educators strive to make education a knowledge-based profession like other professions, the skills and knowledge they gain relate to applying research findings and using data in their decision making. In light of acrimonious public debate about teachers' unions in the United States, it might be assumed that teacher engagement through unions is antithetical to increasing the quality of our schools. But in some high-performing countries, such as Canada and Finland, the teachers' unions have been strong partners in reform.

## Developing Effective School Leaders

School leadership matters—and increasingly so. At the same time that countries are establishing higher, usually national or state standards or curricula to drive their education systems, they are also devolving more authority to the school level for deciding how to meet these more complex educational goals. When an education system's performance is weak, strong government intervention is usually needed. However, moving a system from good to great entails going beyond top-down policy prescriptions to a focus on building the capacity and creativity of schools and generating a professional culture in which best practice is codified and shared.

This trend—together with the evidence that weak school leadership leads to poor performance and high teacher turnover and that high-performing principals can lead to large-scale improvement—has made recruiting and training effective principals and head teachers a new priority in many countries. The roles played by school leaders are also changing. "The job used to be bells, buildings, budgets, and buses; now the pendulum has swung to instructional leadership" (Barber, Whelan, & Clark, 2010, p. 6). According to an international review of the literature by OECD (2008), there are four types of leadership responsibilities that are linked to improved student outcomes:

- Supporting, evaluating, and developing teacher quality as a key to student success.
- Setting school goals for student performance, measuring progress, and making improvements.
- Strategic use of resources to focus all activities on improving teaching and learning.
- Partnering with communities, social agencies, and universities to support the development of the child.

Of these, the single greatest impact comes from promoting teachers' learning and development.

Many countries are establishing new institutions to provide training that is different from traditional administrator programs. Like leadership development in other sectors of the economy, these programs focus on early identification of people with the right personal traits to become leaders and a combination of mentoring and apprenticeship in schools with formal training programs. Once a principal is in position, ongoing peer support is provided through networks and clusters of schools. England's National College of School Leadership is a good example of an approach that combines programs for aspiring leaders and peer support mechanisms for new head teachers (principals) in their first two years of service. The National College program, which is partly online and partly residential, has been extensively evaluated and refined since its founding in 2000. After it was established that graduates of this program outperformed other head teachers, it became mandatory for all prospective school heads (Hopkins, 2007). As another example, China has two high-level, university-based centers for school leadership: one for primary schools, at Beijing Normal University, and one for secondary schools, at East China Normal University in Shanghai. These centers run extensive executive training sessions for current principals based on leadership training practices in other sectors and other countries. High-performing principals in China can take on leadership responsibilities with other schools in their city, as well.

In Canada, Ontario developed a new framework for leadership development starting in 2005, as part of its efforts to build capacity to raise achievement in literacy and numeracy and to reduce the dropout rate. The Ontario Leadership Framework and Principals' Qualification Plan changed the expectations for principals from administrator to instructional leader, and supporting the instructional core became the focus of preparation. All principals and vice principals receive two years of mentoring in each role. Principals, in consultation with their school boards, are required to set a number of challenging but achievable goals and are evaluated based on their achievement of those goals. Each school board also receives funding from the ministry to develop a leadership succession and talent development plan so that momentum is not lost when principals leave.

Australia, which created a national curriculum for the first time in 2009, accompanied it with the establishment of the Australian Institute for Teaching and School Leadership (AITSL) in 2010. The institute's goal is to "provide leadership for the nation, states and territories in promoting excellence in the professions of teaching and school leadership" by creating national professional standards and fostering high-quality professional development (AITSL, n.d.). The new standards for principals are designed to provide a framework for professional learning; to guide self-reflection and self-assessment; to help to prepare, develop, and support principals for leading 21st century schools; and to inform the development of processes for selecting and appraising aspiring and practicing principals.

Finland, as it has in many other aspects of its education system, has taken a different approach. Finnish schools tend to be small, and principals, all of whom are former teachers, act as lead teachers rather than managers. Principals lead not by focusing on performance outcomes but by creating the conditions that produce achievement—a common mission, excellent teachers, and distributed collegial leadership (Hargreaves, Halasz, & Ponti, 2007). As with teachers, school principals are not assessed or ranked based on their or their school's effectiveness. Instead, the ministry uses sample surveys of schools to check that all schools are meeting general standards.

Singapore's approach to leadership is modeled on that of modern corporations. Indeed, schools are viewed as medium-sized enterprises, with similar needs for performance but a more complex group of stakeholders. The key in Singapore is not just the nature of the training but the whole approach to identifying and developing talent (Ng, 2008a). This approach differs from that of the United States, where a teacher can apply to train as a principal or school head and later apply for a position in a school. In Singapore, young teachers are continually assessed for their leadership potential and given opportunities to demonstrate and learn—for example, by serving on committees—then being promoted to head of department at a relatively young age. These teachers are moved into middle management and then, with accompanying experiences and training, into assistant principal roles, often while still in their 30s. If individuals do well in those roles, they have several rounds of interviews with senior ministry officials and go through a two-day leadership situational exercise, a simulation designed to gauge their leadership competency and readiness. Once selected, they spend six months at the Leaders in Education program at the National Institute of Education. The focus of principal training is on innovation and school transformation.

## The Singapore Leaders in Education Programme

The Leaders in Education Programme (LEP) is a six-month, full-time program for educators who are chosen based on their performance and potential for school leadership. Participants' fees are paid by the government, and they receive full salary during the program. The LEP aims to produce school leaders "with the capability to transform schools to be innovative learning communities that nurture innovative students and teachers in an economy driven by knowledge and learning" (Ng, 2008a, p. 237). Guided by a social constructivist philosophy that deems knowledge creation a group interactive process rather than an individual one, the program focuses on three broad areas:

*continued*

**The Singapore Leaders in Education Programme** (*continued*)

- *Knowledge content.* Interactive discussions are intended to spark critical thinking and professional dialogue on issues such as maximizing organizational performance, organizational strategies and identity, e-learning environments and culture, new curriculum and assessment design, creating a vision, and leading a team. A two-week overseas visit challenges participants' thinking about education; following their travel, they must present a review of key lessons to others.
- *Knowledge creation.* Learning groups take on independent projects such as the Future School project, in which groups of six participants are asked to scan future trends and propose a detailed design of a school that can address the needs of Singapore in 15 years' time. The resulting plan, which includes mission; curriculum, pedagogy, and assessment; and a professional development and management model, is presented in public to NIE faculty and Singapore superintendents.
- *Knowledge application.* Each participant is attached to a school for six months of their training and must plan and launch an innovation that is of value to that school.

When I asked Professor Lee Sing Kong, head of the National Institute of Education, why Singapore uses a "select then train" model rather than a "train then select" one, he said that while the U.S. approach is workable, it carries a higher risk. Singapore is very confident that they have the best possible leaders for their schools and that there is a wide range of inputs into their selection. Once trained, principals may be transferred periodically among schools and sometimes into the Ministry of Education as part of Singapore's continuous improvement strategy.

Simply devolving responsibility to schools and giving them more autonomy will not produce increased learning and achievement without dramatically different types of training and support for school leaders. High-performing countries are also creating leadership teams with senior teachers to support the school leader in creating a "thinking school." This is an area of considerable ferment around the world, including in the United States. It is too soon for research to have established empirically whether these new leadership development models work, but they are increasingly seen as key to turning around struggling schools and ramping up achievement on a broad scale.

## Lessons Learned About Effective Teaching and School Leadership

As countries face the challenges of a global knowledge economy that requires them to develop higher levels of knowledge and new capacities in their increasingly diverse students, they are focusing intently on the centrality of teachers to those goals. There is an acknowledgment of the need to respect and reward good teaching. But if the quality of an education system cannot exceed the quality of its teachers, the quality of teachers and of teaching depends on the human resource system that is in place to draw good teachers to the field and support effective practice. High-performing systems focus on ways to attract high-quality candidates into the profession; increase the effectiveness of teacher preparation and modernize it to include 21st century skills and a more global perspective; develop effective systems of teacher professional development, collaboration, and appraisal to deepen student engagement and raise academic performance; ensure that good teachers are available in lower-income rural or urban areas; create career ladders and new leadership roles for the best teachers; and make a quantum leap in the training of principals and head teachers who can drive continuous improvement and transformation in schools.

Educational practices cannot simply be copied wholesale from one country to another; they need to be adapted to different cultural and political settings. But high-performing countries such as those featured in this book have the following things in common: (1) they invest seriously in the human capital of their system as the key to success; (2)

they focus on the instructional core and student outcomes, broadly defined; (3) they have created talent identification and development practices similar to those in the most productive industries; and (4) they have established universal systems for continuous improvement. What international benchmarking can do for every country is help speed up change by providing models of what is happening elsewhere. Each country has some pieces of the whole and can look to others for ideas on the rest.

None of the policies and practices reviewed in this chapter is unknown in the United States. We have pockets of excellence and examples of most of these practices somewhere in the country. But we have not brought together and applied world-class human resource practices in order to raise the academic achievement of schools in a systematic way. We urgently need to do this. Other countries spend a higher proportion of their educational dollar on classroom teachers than the United States does, but this often requires them to make trade-offs in terms of class size, special services, facilities, or administrative overhead. In a decentralized education system like that of the United States, it may not be possible to revamp human resource policies and funding at the national level, but a state or a city could implement and adapt these best practices, work with the relevant stakeholders to make the trade-offs, and create a comprehensive human resources management system that would ensure every student a good teacher and every school a great leader.

 **Reflection Questions**

This review of international best practices suggests a framework of questions that American educators in states, districts, schools, and teacher preparation institutions should reflect on as they ask themselves how we can develop a world-class educator workforce for the future.

1. What is the caliber of teachers in your school? District? State? Do you have shortages in particular areas or subjects?

2. How is the teaching profession viewed by university students and recent graduates in your region of the country?

3. Could a recruitment campaign be mounted to attract more students of high academic caliber who also have a passion for teaching and a commitment to students?

4. How rigorous are the selection processes into teacher training in your state? What competencies do these teacher training institutions produce, and should these competencies be improved or updated?

5. How does starting compensation compare with salaries for other graduates? How else could teaching be made an attractive profession? Could teacher dollars be allocated in some other ways?

6. Does every new teacher receive mentoring/coaching from a master teacher for at least a year?

7. Do you have a teacher appraisal program that is credible to teachers so that every teacher knows his or her particular strengths and weaknesses and has access to effective professional development to improve?

8. Does your school, district, or state have a systematic and universal professional development and collaboration plan for achieving your key academic goals?

9. Does your school or district have a career ladder that enables the best teachers to play leadership roles in school reform and teacher development?

10. How could the recruitment and training of school leaders be significantly improved in your region to create an environment for effective teaching and ramp up achievement?

# 5

# MODERNIZING CURRICULUM, INSTRUCTION, AND ASSESSMENT

The schools for today and yesterday are not the schools we need for tomorrow. Instead we need new mindsets, processes, strategies and new paradigms for instructional leadership. It surprises us that as the world outside changes, the education system can remain static.
**—Ashok Ganguly, Former Chairman of India's Central Board of Secondary Education**

We all have a tendency to think that the curriculum that was in place when we went to school ought to be the curriculum of today. This is comfortable for everyone—teachers, academic experts, and parents. But just as the 19th century school curriculum of the agricultural era gave way to a more scientific and technical curriculum after the industrial revolution (Zhao, 2009), so the hyperdigital and global world of the 21st century will demand different knowledge and skills from our students if they are to be successful.

One of the most striking ways in which international benchmarking has already influenced American educational thinking is through the idea of high universal standards. State commissioners of education with whom I have visited high-performing education systems in Europe and Asia have been impressed by the fact that high-performing countries have higher and more universal standards for what students should know and be able to do than the United States does. And starting in 2008, the Council of Chief State School Officers (CCSSO), the National Governors Association (NGA), and Achieve, Inc., joined together to develop the voluntary Common Core state standards in math and reading that are benchmarked to those of other countries. Forty-four states and the District of Columbia have adopted these standards so far. This chapter discusses the development of the Common Core standards and their implications for our schools.

Beyond the creation of internationally benchmarked standards in literacy and math, there is a much broader and more fundamental discussion going on—all around the world—about what knowledge and skills are most important in global, innovation-oriented societies and economies. The world is changing at breakneck speed. How can we, as educators, best prepare our students for the jobs of the future, many of which have not even been invented yet? What will our students need to be successful citizens and leaders not only in their own communities but in the nation and the world? What are the key trends and issues that should influence what is taught? How should curriculum and instruction in the 21st century be different than in the 20th century, and how are other countries addressing this question?

Assessment, too, needs a major overhaul. The United States' approach to assessment has been very different from that in high-performing countries. Recognizing that overreliance on simple multiple-choice tests has been one of the factors reducing the quality of American education, a revolution in how we assess student learning is brewing, drawing in part on international approaches.

## The Development of "World-Class" Standards

When American public education began in the 19th century, states created a system of *local* school districts and school boards, and these local boards decided most of the content of schooling. In the late 20th century, *states* began to exert more influence by setting academic standards for students in different subjects and sometimes grade levels.

Still, there is enormous variation in expectations for what students should know and be able to do—among different states, among districts within states, and even within the same school. This kind of regional variation was tolerable when students grew up and lived their whole lives in the same local communities. But today, when a student from Missouri is just as likely to end up working in New York, North Carolina, or California for a company that may sell in markets all over the world, it is totally outmoded. It is obviously important for students to appreciate their local and regional heritage and history, but modern math and science and superior literacy skills are the same whether a student is in Mississippi or Montana. The wide discrepancies among state standards and proficiency cut scores are one of the reasons U.S. performance on international tests is so low. More importantly, it means that students across the United States are not equally prepared for college and the labor market; the quality of education they receive is too heavily determined by their zip code.

In fact, there has been a long history of unsuccessful efforts to create *national* standards. In 1959, President Dwight Eisenhower called for national goals in education, including standards. In 1983, under President Ronald Reagan, the report *A Nation at Risk* sounded the alarm about the lack of rigor of educational standards and decried the "rising tide of mediocrity" in American schools. In 1989, President George H. W. Bush convened state governors in Charlottesville, Virginia, where they agreed on the first national education goals in U.S. history. Bush also paid for the development of voluntary American achievement tests, but Congress was critical of the history standards, and that effort was defeated. In 1994, the Clinton administration passed the Goals 2000: Educate America Act, which gave grants to states and set up a federal structure for national standards. But distrust of the federal government led to opposition from states, and the development of those standards was not funded. It is no wonder that national standards came to be considered a political lightning rod, or in the words of President Richard Nixon, "one of the great bugaboos of education" (Schmidt, Houang, & Shakrani, 2009).

In 2002, President George W. Bush's No Child Left Behind Act (NCLB) promoted nationwide testing but neither national standards nor national tests. NCLB required both schools and states to submit annual progress reports. However, when these state reports were compared against states' performance on the National Assessment of Educational Progress (NAEP), a periodic assessment conducted by the U.S. Department of Education, it became clear that there were huge variations in standards and proficiency scores among states and that some states were actually "dumbing down" their proficiency levels to meet the requirements of NCLB. This irrationality and inconsistency, combined with growing educational excellence in other countries, have created a huge momentum for reform.

What makes the current effort to create high universal standards different from efforts undertaken in the past is that now, the push is coming from states, not the federal government, and it is happening in a context of increasing alarm about the poor and stagnant showing of U.S. students in international comparisons. In 2008, the report *Benchmarking for Success: Ensuring U.S. Students Receive a World-Class Education* (NGA et al., 2008) argued that not only was America losing its historic edge in education, but the poor performance and, especially, the large gaps between the scores of students from different socioeconomic groups were hurting us economically and socially. It recommended that the United States should emulate top-performing nations and "upgrade its state standards by adopting a common core of internationally bench-marked standards in math and language arts for grades K–12 to ensure that students are equipped with the necessary knowledge and skills to be globally competitive" (p. 24).

Under the auspices of CCSSO, NGA, and Achieve, committees of teachers and academic experts were asked to draft standards for English language arts and mathematics. Because earlier efforts at creating standards in the 1980s and 1990s had developed lists that were far too long for a teacher to cover in a single year, the Common Core State Standards Initiative (CCSSI) focused more narrowly on what skills and knowledge students need to handle credit-bearing college courses and workforce training programs. The goal was to establish "fewer, clearer, higher" standards for college- and career-readiness. The committees drew on ACT and College Board data, reviewed current state standards, examined college work samples, and looked at the expectations of the highest-performing countries on international assessments (PISA and TIMSS). Once the CCSSI had drafted its standards, expert working groups developed progressions of knowledge and skills students needed to learn from kindergarten through 12th grade in order to meet standards by the time they graduate from high school.

According to William Schmidt, a researcher who studies math and science curricula around the world, there are three critical instructional commonalities between countries whose students excel in science and math: focus, rigor, and coherence. In terms of focus, Schmidt's research showed that high-performing nations cover fewer topics in each grade level, allowing students to master the key concepts before moving on, whereas the U.S. math curriculum covers a large number of topics in every grade level, producing a curriculum that is "a mile wide and an inch deep." In 8th grade, when many American students are still studying fractions and arithmetic, students in other nations are learning algebra, geometry, and trigonometry. In addition, math standards in high-performing countries lay out "an orderly progression of topics that follow the logic of the discipline, allowing thorough and deep coverage of content." By contrast, many state standards "resemble an arbitrary laundry list of topics, resulting in too much repetition across grades" (Schmidt, 2005).

The CCSSI's drafts were released for public comment in 2009. Interest was high, and 10,000 comments were received covering a wide range of issues, including the balance between content and skills and the best ways to prepare students for algebra. The standards and comments were then reviewed and revised by an independent validation committee. Somehow, the committees managed to overcome the contentious debates about curriculum that have long riven both disciplines. The final Common Core standards for English K–5 and 6–12; literacy in history/social studies, science, and technical subjects; and mathematics K–8 and high school were released in June 2010. By January 2011, an astonishing 44 states and the District of Columbia—80 percent of the public school population—had committed to the standards (see www. corestandards.org), and the standards also received the endorsement of many big city school districts. States that adopt the Common Core standards have agreed that these will comprise 85 percent of instructional standards in math and English statewide, leaving 15 percent of standards up to local selection.

The Common Core standards differ from most current state standards in a number of ways. The English language arts standards emphasize text complexity, proceeding from the belief that the texts many students are reading today are not of sufficient complexity to prepare them for college and career demands. The English standards also call for students to read a wide array of classic and contemporary literature and challenging informational texts, but they defer most of the choice of such texts to the local level. Sample texts are provided to help teachers and parents understand the level of text being recommended. The standards refocus high school writing primarily on argument and the use of evidence to make a case in writing, as written analysis is fundamental to success in college. Samples of student writing are also provided to illustrate performance levels. Research, listening, and speaking skills are emphasized at all grade levels, and, since technology will be central to learning and work in the 21st century, media analysis and production are also addressed.

The Common Core standards for math draw on the lessons from high-performing countries by giving greater focus to the curriculum, allowing teachers and students more time to develop mastery of concepts rather than having to spend large amounts of time reviewing the same concepts year after year. In the elementary grades, the Common Core math standards emphasize a solid foundation in whole numbers, addition, subtraction, multiplication, division, fractions, and decimals. The middle school curriculum uses hands-on learning in geometry, probability, and statistics so that students will be prepared for algebra in grade 8. And both the middle and high school standards call on students to practice applying mathematical thinking to real-world issues and challenges. The Common Core math standards thus emphasize depth of understanding and ability to apply math to new situations, as college students and employees must do (James B. Hunt Jr. Institute,

2011). The standards and information on their development and status in states can all be found at www.corestandards.org.

The Thomas Fordham Institute, an organization that has reviewed state standards periodically since 1997 for rigor and clarity, compared the Common Core standards with all 50 existing state standards and concluded that the Common Core's English language arts (ELA) standards are clearer and more rigorous than the ELA standards in 37 states and equivalent to those in 11 other states. Their review also concluded that the Common Core math standards were better than those in 39 states (Carmichael, Wilson, Finn, Winkler, & Palmieri, 2009). Although much work remains to be done, it seems that the idea of common high standards for all students, regardless of where they live, has achieved widespread support across the political spectrum as a significant step toward raising student achievement to international levels and reducing achievement gaps.

However, high universal standards are just the first step. They must be accompanied by high-quality content, whether in books or online; alignment of teacher preparation programs; intensive professional development; and sophisticated assessments—just as they are in high-performing countries.

## New Skills for Global Innovation Societies

The Common Core standards discussion is one part of a much broader and more fundamental debate about what knowledge and skills are most important to prepare our students for the 21st century. It is not only the United States that fears falling behind! Leaders everywhere are concerned that education systems are too slow to keep pace with the transformative changes taking place in contemporary economies and societies.

Children entering kindergarten today, if they stay in school, will graduate high school in about 2024 and will be in the workforce until 2070. The education they receive today must prepare them for that lifetime. Are we preparing students for the world of the future or the world of the past? Just as army generals have a tendency to fight the last war, we educators often educate students for the demands of today or even yesterday rather than for the demands of tomorrow. No one has a crystal ball to see the future exactly, but there are certain recognizable trends that seem likely to be major influences on societies and economies as the future unfolds and that call for different kinds of knowledge and skills. What are these trends? And how does what we are doing to respond to them compare with the actions of other countries? These are issues that are central to educational debates throughout the world, so educators and innovators in the United States have both a lot to share with their international peers and a lot to learn.

In my view, global knowledge economies and societies share the following characteristics. They are

- *Science and technology-based*: requiring scientific and technological literacy.
- *Resource-challenged*: in need of critical thinking about sustainable economies,
- *Globally interdependent*: requiring global knowledge and skills as a core competence.
- *Innovation-driven*: placing high value on creativity and knowing how to learn.

Each of these attributes has implications for curriculum and instruction.

## Ensuring Scientific and Technological Literacy

Over the past 40 years, the mix of jobs in the U.S. economy has changed dramatically. Manufacturing jobs, which employed 50 percent of workers in the 1950s, now account for only 10 percent—a decline due as much to technological changes as to jobs moving offshore (Levy & Murnane, 2004). As a result, whole neighborhoods and cities have become rust belts. Aspects of some services such as accounting and medical laboratory work are also declining for similar reasons. At the same time, whole new industries are being created, often involving the convergence of a number of disciplines such as computing, engineering, life sciences, and design. In the near future we will have robots, smart devices, gene-based products, nanotechnology—things unimaginable a few years ago.

In this new world, all students, not just the science geeks, will need a deeper understanding of science and technology. And yet, two-thirds of Americans do not understand DNA, despite its increasing prevalence in legal trials, and half believe falsely that antibiotics kill viruses (National Academy of Sciences, 2007). Clearly, American workers with strong math and science skills are necessary to fuel our nation's capacity to create new ideas, products, and services. But all Americans, no matter what their line of work, will need a deeper understanding of the STEM fields (science, technology, engineering, and mathematics) to be able to understand and apply scientific information in their daily lives at home, school, and work. As citizens of the 21st century, they will need to understand the difference between science and pseudoscience, and be able to make informed decisions on issues from high-speed trains to stem cell research to alternative energy solutions.

Why don't U.S. students stack up well in science compared with their international peers? Much of the answer lies in the kind of big systems issues discussed in previous chapters. Other countries have more qualified teachers; high common standards with less variation between regions; more effective intervention to reduce the size of socioeconomic achievement gaps; and greater alignment between standards, curriculum, teacher training, and assessment. But there are also issues that are specific to science teaching and learning.

Visitors to schools in high-performing countries, myself included, recognize straightaway that science and math play a much more central role in these education systems and that the expectations for the amounts and levels of science and math that students will study are considerably higher than in the United States. In China, for example, all students are expected to take a strong core curriculum in math and science, including algebra, geometry, biology, physics, and chemistry, in order to graduate from high school. As a result, girls as well as boys do well in science. In the United States, by comparison, not only do educational standards vary widely among different educational jurisdictions, but students are allowed to choose among several levels of courses, and many opt out of more advanced courses.

Added to that, our science curricula, like our math curricula, are broad and shallow. "While American students are learning the nomenclature of human anatomy, students in other countries are learning how body parts work. They learn how you see while we learn what the parts of the eye are," said William Schmidt (2008). Bruce Alberts (2009), former head of the National Academy of Sciences, believes that our current approach is turning kids off to science. "What is taught in schools today is a caricature of science," he says, and scientists are themselves partly to blame (p. 39). In the 1990s, the National Academy of Sciences itself produced a set of recommended national science standards. However, these standards were produced by expert committees of scientists from different disciplines, and the resulting sets of standards were enormous. The problem was exacerbated by the state textbook adoption process. To meet the very detailed standards issued by some states, textbook publishers produced books to satisfy the needs of as many states as possible. The results were voluminous—the mile wide, inch deep phenomenon again. With so much to cover, the books developed a heavy focus on scientific terms. "We adults have somehow let science education be reduced to the memorization of key science terms," Alberts observed. In addition, because states typically use simple, low-cost, multiple-choice tests that can be rapidly scored, it is much easier to test for science words than to test for science understanding. These factors have defined what science education means on a day-to-day basis in many of our schools: rote memorization of terms.

Educators and scientists alike recognize the urgent need to change this situation and focus on building conceptual knowledge and application, developing skills and processes, problem solving, and practicing inquiry, rather than on memorizing long lists of terms and formulae. Teachers know that the pursuit of inquiry—the approach scientists use to study the natural world—is the best way to ignite students' curiosity and passion for the subject. Indeed, the greater use of inquiry methods in our best classrooms is widely admired around the world. However, the constraints of voluminous textbooks and low-level assessments have all but pushed it out of many classrooms.

In 2010, a commission convened by the Carnegie Corporation of New York and the Institute for Advanced Study issued its report, *The Opportunity Equation: Transforming Math and Science Education for Citizenship and the Global Economy.* It called for the development of a set of core standards for science education that focus on this inquiry approach. Subsequently, the National Research Council, the operating arm of the National Academy of Sciences, issued a report in 2011 that outlined a new conceptual framework for science education. It also called for paring the curriculum to focus on core ideas and teaching students how to approach and solve problems rather than just memorizing factual information (National Research Council, 2011). Following the publication of this framework, several key science organizations, including the National Science Teachers Association, American Association for the Advancement of Science, and National Academy of Sciences, working with Achieve, will develop a Common Core–like "next generation" set of science standards in 2012 for states to consider adopting. The new science standards will take into account significant changes that have taken place in science and technology over the past 15years, the science standards of high-performing countries, and the increasing importance of engineering. Above all, the new standards will emphasize the importance of students learning science by doing science (Achieve, Inc., 2010). However, as *The Opportunity Equation* also pointed out, to have a widespread impact on American education, these new standards will need to be accompanied by the creation of high-quality assessments that match the standards and by strengthening the human resource system of states and school districts to recruit, retain, and deploy a corps of highly qualified science and math teachers.

Clearly changes of significant magnitude will be needed to ensure that American students acquire the scientific and technological literacy to equip them for the global knowledge economy. These will take some time to be implemented. In the meantime, here are some low-cost ideas for schools that want to redress the balance in their science teaching:

- Reduce the focus on memorizing scientific terms and number of labs and other inquiry-oriented projects. MIT' (https://wikis.mit.edu/confluence/display/ILAB2/Home) offers ways for students to access remote laboratories online.
- Have math and science teachers review the publically released math and science PISA questions (www.pisa.oecd.org/dataoecd/ 47/23/41943106.pdf) and incorporate some of them into lessons.
- Create a collaborative science experiment with a school in another country so your students can learn what it is like to do science in global teams. Try NASA's GLOBE Program (http://globe.gov/) or iearn (http://us.iearn.org) to get started.

## Promoting Critical Thinking About Sustainable Economies

Until the last few years Americans took cheap and limitless resources for granted. But steep rises in energy and raw material prices in recent years remind us that resources are finite. And by 2020, a further 30 percent increase in the global consumption of resources like oil, metals, water, and food is predicted (McKinsey Global Institute, 2009). Former Vice President Al Gore's documentary *An Inconvenient Truth* brought home the message that global warming, linked to our societies releasing carbon at rates faster than Earth can absorb, is causing the Arctic ice cover to shrink, glaciers on three continents to retreat, and sea levels to rise. Extreme weather conditions—both floods and drought—have reduced agricultural yields and are leading to the extinction of species, the spread of life-threatening diseases, and the possibility of mass migrations. All of the systems on which life on Earth depends are declining.

Developing a global consensus on how to respond to these crises is not easy, especially among countries in very different stages of economic development. But global agreements are slowly emerging, and governments are taking their own actions. The European Union adopted a climate and energy package in 2008, and Australia and Brazil did the same in 2009. Industries are developing new business models to bring sustainability into their bottom line, and clean energy is a huge new sector of economic growth. China, which along with the United States is the world's biggest contributor to carbon, has also become the world's largest manufacturer of wind turbines and solar panels.

The knowledge, skills, and attitudes that drive behavior are learned when people are young. As education systems worldwide are adding environmental literacy or sustainability education to their school curricula, PISA science surveys in 2006 show that U.S. students, like students in all OECD countries, are very aware of environmental hazards. Students with the deepest knowledge of science had the highest level of environmental awareness and sense of responsibility for sustainability. We know that American students are already very interested in these issues and are waiting for the curriculum to catch up, so this is an area where strong student engagement is likely.

There has been progress in American schools over the past five years. The growing awareness of the dangers of climate change has created public support for changes in curriculum. Some states have enacted environmental or sustainability initiatives, and others are adding environmental literacy to science or social studies standards.

Many schools have been integrating environmental education on their own. For example:

• Elementary schools are exploring the land use patterns of their local communities and their impact on the ecosystem and are planting gardens to study water usage.

• Middle schools are creating multidisciplinary units by bringing together science, social studies, English, and math teachers to examine environmental issues.

• High schools are offering capstone projects like the Education Development Center's Biocomplexity and the Habitable Planet project (see www.edc.org/projects/).

• Students are using energy modeling software to analyze their school's energy use and research how to retrofit their buildings for conservation.

• Many schools are working with farms to increase the amount of fresh, seasonal, and organic food served in cafeterias.

• Free curricular materials and projects are available from a wide variety of organizations, including the National Science Foundation; the

National Institutes of Health; the Environmental Protection Agency; the GEMS project at the Lawrence Hall of Science in Berkeley, California; and the Cloud Institute for Sustainability Education.

 • Some American schools are participating in international sustainability projects such as the United Nations' Water for Life project or the National Science Foundation's Global Challenge, in which U.S. and international high school students work together to create solutions to global warming.

Unfortunately, budget constraints and the heavy focus on testing in traditional subjects have made it hard for an interdisciplinary approach to studying sustainability to flourish on a broad scale. States need to be more explicit in their state content and performance standards and assessments, and sustainability concepts need to be included in teacher training and professional development opportunities (Federico & Cloud, 2009). Overall, we need to accelerate the pace of change in American curriculum and instruction to equip our next generation to think and act on the challenge of our very survival.

What do teachers and schools need to provide? According to Jamie Cloud, a leader in sustainability education, in order to have the knowledge, skills, and habits of mind to create the shift toward a sustainable future, students need to do the following:

 • Understand the dynamics of complex living systems and how they change, and have the concepts and tools of systems thinking to address the choices that will affect their future.

 • Understand the theories of sustainable economics and how individual behavior can contribute to the health of the planet.

 • Recognize the interdependence of living things through a healthy Commons, and assume responsibility for caring for the Commons.

 • Be able to work with others of different backgrounds to design and implement actions that serve their community (Cloud, 2010).

## Developing Global Knowledge and Skills

The world into which today's students will graduate is interconnected as never before. Companies manufacture goods around the clock and around the world. Ideas and events traverse the Internet in seconds. A financial crisis in the United States affects farmers in Africa, and pollution in China influences the air in Los Angeles. Our schools must therefore prepare our students for a world where the opportunities for success require the ability to *compete, connect, and cooperate* on a global scale. Both as workers and as citizens, our students will need to be able to relate effectively to citizens of other nations and other cultures.

Our curricula have not traditionally emphasized knowledge of the world outside our borders. Surveys by Asia Society found that 25 percent of college-bound students could not name the ocean between California and Asia, 37 percent could not find China on a map, and 80 percent did not know that India is the world's largest democracy. Surveys by the National Geographic Society found that U.S. students were next to last in knowledge of international affairs compared with students in 14 other industrialized countries. And the 2010 National Assessment of Educational Progress found that fewer than one in three American students are proficient in geography (NAEP, 2011). In other developed countries, world geography and world history are standard parts of the core curriculum for all students.

Language learning will also be more important than before. English will continue to be a major global lingua franca, but the use of other languages like Chinese, Arabic, and Spanish is increasing on the Internet and in business. In this area, the United States is far behind other developed countries, where learning a second language is part of the core curriculum starting in the elementary grades—when cognitive science shows that language learning is more effective—and continuing for five years or more. In the United States, although the proportion of high school students taking a foreign language remained relatively stable from 1997 to 2008, the proportion of U.S. students taking a foreign language at the middle school level declined from 75 percent to 58 percent, and at the elementary level, it dropped from 31 percent to 19 percent (American Council on the Teaching of Foreign Languages, 2011). This decline may be attributable to NCLB squeezing out foreign language instruction in favor of subjects emphasized in high-stakes accountability testing (Rhodes & Pufahl, 2009). By contrast, in China, all children are now learning a second language—primarily English. In Australia, one-quarter of students now study one of four Asian languages in addition to the European languages that have long been offered. In Europe, studying two languages beyond students' home language is now recommended. Learning other languages not only gives insight into the cultures associated with that language, but also develops the skills that will enable students to better understand and interact with representatives of other cultures more generally. It is no surprise that global companies are looking to hire graduates from these parts of the world who have these desirable language and cross-cultural skills. In fact, language learning is a central part of what high-performing nations are doing to make their students and societies globally competitive (National Research Council, 2007).

The Committee for Economic Development (2006) cites a survey of U.S. corporations that estimated that companies lose more than $2 billion a year due to inadequate linguistic and cross-cultural guidance for their employees in working with their foreign counterparts. The report went on to say that "to compete successfully in the global marketplace, U.S.-based multinationals as well as small businesses must market products to customers around the globe and work effectively with foreign employees and business partners. [U.S.] firms increasingly need employees with knowledge of foreign languages and cultures" (pp. 1–2). This working knowledge of foreign languages and cultures will become ever more necessary since, according to many economists, 50 percent of GDP growth over the next 20 years will take place outside the developed world and particularly in the large and expanding urbanized middle classes of the BRIC countries—Brazil, Russia, India, and China.

But economic costs and job opportunities are not the only reason for reconceptualizing our curriculum for the new global context. The most pressing challenges of our time know no boundaries. The effects of poverty, injustice, and lack of education elsewhere spill across borders. Conflict generates international migration (Reimers, 2009). Virtually every major health, environmental, and human security issue Americans face—from environmental degradation, to pandemic diseases, to energy and water shortages, to terrorism and weapons proliferation—can only be solved through international collaboration. As the line between domestic and international affairs blurs, what we do affects others and what others do affects us. We need to give our students the knowledge and tools to act as citizens in the world of the future.

Even within the boundaries of the United States, daily life in communities and workplaces increasingly involves interacting and working with individuals from different backgrounds. According to the U.S. Census Bureau (2008), the population identifying as Asian is projected to increase from 15.5 million in 2008 to 40.6 million in 2050, and its share of the total U.S. population will rise from 5.2 percent to 9.1 percent. The Hispanic population is projected to nearly triple, going from 46.7 million (15 percent of the total population) in 2008 to 132.8 million (30 percent of the total population) in 2050. This increasing diversity is not just a feature of urban schools; suburban and even rural schools are experiencing a degree of ethnic diversity that was rare a generation ago. Understanding and valuing multiple cultures, whether in a domestic or international context, are key to functioning in the world of the 21st century.

Given the imperative to respond to this increasingly global context, our students need a new kind of competence—global competence. Global competence has been defined by a task force of the Council of Chief State School Officers as "the capacity to employ knowledge and skills effectively to understand and participate in an increasingly complex, diverse, and interconnected world" (Boix-Mansilla & Jackson, 2011, p. 12). The capacities that contribute to global competence—or global literacy, as it is sometimes called—involve students developing knowledge of world regions and cultures; skills to frame and investigate global issues and communicate ideas in a variety of cultural contexts; and the attitudes or ethical dispositions to engage with others and see themselves as thoughtful actors in the world. The development of these capacities is not limited to a particular discipline but can be integrated throughout a school's curriculum.

Over the past few years, despite the pressures of high-stakes testing in reading and math, hundreds of schools have begun to redefine their mission to be along the lines of "preparing students for leadership in their communities, the nation, and the world." At the elementary school level, there are a small but growing number of dual-language immersion programs. These are immediately oversubscribed by parents. Chinese language programs have grown an astonishing 60 percent between 2005 and 2010. Secondary schools are bringing a global focus into many subjects, including arts, physical education, career and technical education, and service learning, and are using technology to link their schools to schools in other countries, making their classrooms as wide as the world. Asia Society's International Studies Network, a network of schools serving low-income students, is showing that an engaging, internationally themed program can raise student achievement and graduation rates as well as produce students with global knowledge and skills. These innovations in teaching and learning serve both as inspiration and as practical, achievable models of change.

Take, for example, the John Stanford Elementary School in Seattle. In this public K–5 immersion school, students spend half their day studying math, science, culture, and literacy in their chosen world language, Japanese or Spanish, and the other half of the day learning reading, writing, and social studies in English. International content appears across all curricular areas. A local arts organization provides artists-in-residence to teach students dance, music, and visual art from around the world. Local businesses and the University of Washington have helped with the development of content for the school. Partnerships with schools in Puerta Vallarta, Mexico, and Kobe, Japan, enhance the international dimensions of the school and provide options for language exchange. The school is also a center for new immigrant students and provides English as a second language courses for children and after-school classes for parents. John Stanford combines strong academic results with superior language proficiency, and it has won many awards, inspiring the development of several more internationally themed schools in Seattle.

Or take the Walter Payton College Prep High School in Chicago. This inner-city magnet school, one of Chicago's most ethnically diverse schools, has shown how integrating global content enhances academic excellence. Every student studies a world language for four years and participates in a home-stay exchange with a sister school in China, France, North Africa, Japan, Switzerland, Chile, Italy, or South Africa. Extensive use of videoconferencing connects Payton classrooms to classes in sister schools and to subject matter experts around the world. An array of international visitors, students, and seminars extends the international spirit of the school.

Some states are also beginning to focus on their students' global competence. Utah is a less populous state that is nevertheless positioning itself for success in the global economy. According to Utah State Senator Howard Stephenson, "In this increasingly competitive world, it is critical for Utah students to be able to deliver services and information in various languages and to appreciate the subtleties of doing business in other cultures" (Utah Department of Education, 2011). In 2007, the Utah legislature funded the development of dual-language immersion programs starting in elementary school. The goal is to create 100 such programs in Spanish, Mandarin Chinese, French, and eventually up to eight languages in schools around the state by 2015. Since immersion programs like these are unusual in the United States (although common in Canada, among other countries), Utah shares materials and professional development with schools in other parts of the country that are developing similar programs.

The Asia Society handbooks *Going Global* (2008a, for secondary schools), *Ready for the World* (for elementary schools), *Expanding Horizons* (for after-school programs), and *How to Create a Chinese Language Program in Your School* (all available through http://asiasociety.org) offer practical examples from hundreds of schools in places as different as Vermont, West Virginia, North Carolina, Texas, Florida, Kansas, Wisconsin, Oregon, Oklahoma, and Utah. Schools start their journeys toward becoming global schools in different places and in small ways, but drawing on my research and visits to schools, I have noted six key common elements:

• They create a global vision and culture by revising their mission statements and graduate profiles and creating a school culture that supports international learning.

- They develop an internationally oriented faculty by recr\ teachers with international interests and encouraging teachers to take advantage of study/travel and professional development opportunities.
- They integrate international content into all curriculum areas, bringing a global dimension to science and language arts as well as to social studies and languages.
- They emphasize the learning of world languages, including languages that are less commonly taught.
- They harness technology to tap global information sources, create international collaborations, and offer international courses online.
- They expand student experiences through internationally oriented service learning, internships, and partnerships with schools in other countries.

The ways in which individual schools utilize community resources to link the local to the global demonstrate that teaching and learning about the world is within reach of every type of school (Stewart, 2010/2011). We have the tools and models to help our students succeed in this new global context. We just need to put them to work in all of our schools, not just the pioneering few.

## Promoting Creativity and Learning How to Learn

Innovation is the lifeblood of the 21st century economy. All across the globe, educators are trying to define and produce the new skill set that will be needed in a global knowledge economy where economic growth and jobs are driven by innovation. How do you produce more Silicon Valleys? This is the question everyone is asking. Knowledge is changing, technology is changing, and our understanding of learning is deeper— but schools have remained the same (Jerald, 2009; Partnership for 21st Century Skills, 2009; Wagner, 2008). The old basics are still important, but new basics will be required, including a deeper understanding of academic content, the ability to apply knowledge to new problems, and a set of strategies to enable students to "learn how to learn," be creative, and take control of their own learning. Even countries that perform well on international tests of student achievement have recognized that the exponential pace of change and the enormous amount of information accessible require schools to teach new skills or emphasize different ones.

For example, in the late 1990s, Singapore, under the "Thinking Schools, Learning Nation" rubric, began to move from a school system heavily focused on knowledge transmission to one that also tried to promote creative thinking skills and passion for lifelong learning. More recently, its Curriculum 2015 initiatives have aimed at producing students who are self-directed learners who think critically, contribute actively to innovation, and are "future-ready." Finland is broadening its educational goals to include "21st century citizen skills, including problem-solving, teamwork and entrepreneurship skills, participation and initiative." In Ontario, which has successfully raised basic skills achievement, the Student Work Study and Thinking About Thinking initiatives are aiming to support teachers' capacity to promote higher-order thinking. In Hong Kong, primary school exams have been abolished to allow more active learning in the early grades, and a crucial curriculum document titled "Learning to Learn" (OECD, 2011b) has guided numerous innovations in secondary schools—including the addition of liberal studies in which students define their own interests and design, analyze, and synthesize information about contemporary topics. And several years ago, the European Union defined "learning to learn" as a key competency and is working on new ways to assess it. Most European countries place increasing value on "flexibility, entrepreneurship and personal responsibility. Individuals are expected to be adaptive, but also innovative, creative, self-directed and self-motivated" (Hoskins & Fedrikssson, 2008).

In the United States, these curriculum and instructional directions have become variously known as "21st century skills," "deeper learning," and "higher-order skills." Labor economists emphasize that the skill demands in the U.S. economy are changing rapidly. Computers are increasingly taking over routine work in both blue-collar and white-collar fields. And while low-level service jobs are still a significant part of the economy, the overall trend is toward more cognitively demanding jobs that require expert thinking and complex communication. This includes not only new jobs but also the "upskilling" of traditional occupations like construction and electrical work as buildings and vehicles become "smart" (Levy & Murnane, 2004). In response to fierce global competition, companies are also intently focused on innovation. Indeed, the New Commission on the Skills of the American Workforce, after reviewing extensive research on workforce and global economic trends, concluded that academic knowledge and skills, applied literacies, and critical thinking will not be sufficient for the United States to maintain its competitive edge in the global economy. "The crucial new factor, the one that alone can justify higher wages in this country than in other countries with similar levels of cognitive skills, is creativity and innovation" (National Center on Education and the Economy, 2007).

What are the skills that students need for an innovation-driven economy, and how do we organize schools to promote them? Led by a core group of technology companies, the Partnership for 21st Century Skills argues that students need problem-solving skills, critical-thinking skills, information and technology skills, and self-direction. Other efforts, such as those of the Hewlett Foundation, focus on "deeper learning" (Alliance for Excellent Education, 2011); still others on "higher-order skills." While the lists of proposed 21st century educational outcomes may be slightly different, they all include deeper content knowledge and critical thinking skills combined with soft skills such as teamwork, collaboration, and communication. Critics object that these skills are not new to the 21st century and have always been part of a good education. What is new is that "the skills that have been the province of the few must become universal" (Rotherham & Willingham, 2009, p. 16).

Some of the rhetoric associated with the 21st century skills movement has also been taken to suggest that with so much new knowledge being created, content no longer matters—that ways of knowing information are now more important than information itself. Students have been known to ask, "Why do you need to know that stuff if you can look it up on Google?" However, the debate should not be about content versus skills. Research in cognitive science tells us that knowledge and skills are inextricably intertwined. To think critically and understand the structure of a problem, students need the knowledge that is central to the domain. In fact, they need a *deeper* knowledge of content; Levy and Murnane (2004) talk about "expert thinking" rather than "critical thinking."

So students still need the foundational knowledge of subject matter, often at a higher level. But they also need to be able to do more than simply reproduce that information on a test that requires a single correct answer. They need to be able to apply their subject matter knowledge to real-life situations in postsecondary education or the job market. This greater emphasis on the *application* of knowledge, sometimes known as literacies, is what the PISA assessments have been explicitly designed to measure. In fact, the decision by the member countries of OECD, including the United States, to focus the PISA assessment heavily on applications of knowledge rather than just reproducing the information in the curriculum arose from extensive review of international research on learning as well as the views of ministries of education and employers around the world.

Modern workplaces are organized to have less hierarchy and fewer layers of management, and these "flatter" organizations are generally run through self-managing work teams and increased horizontal collaboration with team members working remotely. This style of organization requires stronger interpersonal and team skills, and individuals have to take more responsibility for defining and carrying out tasks. They also have to take more responsibility for their careers. Jobs no longer last for a lifetime, and employment is offered based primarily on needs and performance (O'Toole & Lawlor, 2006). Workers also have to take more responsibility for their own health care and financial/retirement planning. For all these reasons, self-direction, learning how to learn, and periodically updating one's knowledge and skills are increasingly critical.

A 2006 Conference Board survey of employers identified four competencies that employers viewed as essential for success in the workplace: (1) critical thinking/problem solving, (2) application of information technology, (3) teamwork and collaboration, and (4) creativity/innovation. Interestingly, the Conference Board found that while 73 percent of school superintendents rated high school graduates as proficient at problem solving, only 45 percent of employers did so. This is probably because employers think in terms of problems that have no rule-based solutions. They want employees who can think on their feet and find creative solutions to problems that are unfamiliar and unstructured, and often have no single solution. In terms of schooling, this means that we need to encourage students to work in groups, synthesize, analyze, try, fail, and try again.

There is a lot of discussion these days about the importance of creativity, but what is creativity, and what are the sources of support for its development? According to a review of research on creativity by Adams (2005), creativity requires deep technical expertise in one area and broad knowledge of unrelated areas. It depends on being able to combine disparate elements in new ways and relies heavily on synthesis—the ability to see patterns where others don't. Whereas traditional education has focused on helping students find the right answer to well-structured problems, environments that support creativity permit a lot of failure. Creativity is not a flash of insight but a combination of several key factors:

* *Knowledge:* Deep knowledge of one domain and broad exposure to many areas
* *Creative thinking skills:* Ability to synthesize information in new ways, analyze ideas, and promote practical and creative ideas
* *Motivation:* Curiosity, intrinsic interest, perseverance, willingness to take risks, and comfort with ambiguity
* *Metacognition:* Explicit decision to be creative
* *Environment:* Driven by intrinsic incentives, collaborative, and encouraging risk taking

Many of these constructs will be familiar to educators. Independent thinking, problem solving, and decision making, for example, are part of the advanced skills in Bloom's familiar taxonomy. We also have a lot of research on and good practice examples of how to do inquiry-oriented learning in science, applications in math, critical thinking about literary or subject matter content texts, and imaginative projects in the arts. Indeed, the United States is universally perceived as having a much stronger tradition in these areas than other countries. But in order to be able to create these kinds of learning environments on a far broader scale, we will need clearer definitions of some of these constructs, more research on effective instructional practices, and widespread professional support for teachers to be able to produce these outcomes. And we need to learn how to assess some of these skills—like self-direction, creativity, and innovation—as well as we now assess standard subjects.

## Assessment

For all the talk about new standards, educators know that the real standard is what's on the test. Much as we all decry different aspects of testing, we have to have it—to monitor students' progress, give feedback to teachers, and inform the public. But compared to high-performing countries, the United States has the wrong kind of assessments.

The dominant American testing paradigm is different from the rest of the world in a number of ways. First, we frequently use high-stakes external tests with relatively young children, whereas most countries rely primarily on school-based testing at the elementary level. Second, we rely heavily on frequent, low-cost multiple-choice tests, which tend to measure limited ranges of knowledge and skills and are of little help to teachers seeking to understand students' needs and tailor instruction accordingly. There are concerns that overreliance on "fill in the bubble" assessment encourages schools to focus the curriculum narrowly on lower-order skills, especially for low-income and minority students (Asia Society & CCSSO, 2010). Indeed, some people argue that one reason for American students' poor performance on international assessments is that American students are far more accustomed to recall and fact recognition—a mainstay of multiple-choice testing—than they are to the application and problem-solving that characterize PISA. As an example, see Figure 6 for a comparison of test items taken from the NAEP and OECD's PISA.

Third, American schools feature a confusing array of tests, and in significant volume. The layering-on of tests from the local, state, and national levels forces students to sit for numerous tests, often with conflicting requirements, ever year. Finally, at the secondary level, U.S.

| Figure 6 | A Comparison of Sample Test Items from NAEP and PISA |
| --- | --- |

### NAEP 8th Grade Science Sample Question

1. What two gases make up most of the Earth's atmosphere?

    A. Hydrogen and oxygen

    B. Hydrogen and nitrogen

    C. Oxygen and carbon dioxide

    D. Oxygen and nitrogen

### PISA 2009 Sample Science Question
*The Greenhouse Effect: Fact or Fiction?*

Living things need energy to survive. The energy that sustains life on the Earth comes from the Sun, which radiates energy into space because it is so hot. A tiny proportion of this energy reaches the Earth. The Earth's atmosphere acts like a protective blanket over the surface of our planet, preventing the variations in temperature that would exist in an airless world.

Most of the radiated energy coming from the Sun passes through the Earth's atmosphere. The Earth absorbs some of this energy, and some is reflected back from the Earth's surface. Part of this reflected energy is absorbed by the atmosphere.

As a result of this the average temperature above the Earth's surface is higher than it would be if there were no atmosphere. The Earth's atmosphere has the same effect as a greenhouse, hence the term *greenhouse effect*.

The greenhouse effect is said to have become more pronounced during the 20th century. It is a fact that the average temperature of the Earth's atmosphere has increased. In newspapers and periodicals the increased carbon dioxide emission is often stated as the main source of the temperature rise in the 20th century.

A student named André becomes interested in the possible relationship between the average temperature of the Earth's atmosphere and the carbon dioxide emission on the Earth. In a library he comes across the following two graphs:

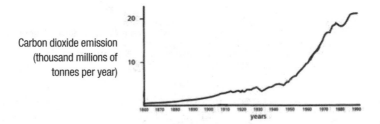

*continued*

| Figure 6 | A Comparison of Sample Test Items from NAEP and PISA (continued) |
|---|---|

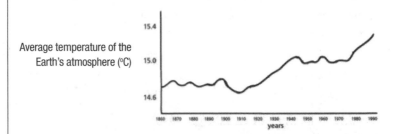

Average temperature of the Earth's atmosphere (°C)

André concludes from these two graphs that it is certain that the increase in the average temperature of the Earth's atmosphere is due to the increase in the carbon dioxide emission.

**Question 5.1**
What is it about the graphs that supports André's conclusion?

**Question 5.2**
Another student, Jeanne, disagrees with André's conclusion. She compares the two graphs and says that some parts of the graphs do not support his conclusion. Give an example of a part of the graphs that does not support André's conclusion. Explain your answer.

**Question 5.3**
André persists in his conclusion that the average temperature rise of the Earth's atmosphere is caused by the increase in the carbon dioxide emission. But Jeanne thinks that his conclusion is premature. She says: "Before accepting this conclusion you must be sure that other factors that could influence the greenhouse effect are constant."

Name one of the factors that Jeanne means.

*Source:* NAEP sample question from the U.S. Department of Education, Institute of Education Sciences, National Center for Education Statistics, National Assessment of Educational Progress (NAEP), 2005 Science Assessment, Grade 8; PISA material from Science Unit 5: Greenhouse, "The greenhouse effect: fact or fiction?" OECD (2009), *Take the Test: Sample Questions from OECD's PISA Assessments, PISA.* Paris: OECD Publishing. http://dx.doi.org/10.1787/9789264050815-en. Reprinted with permission.

high school exit exams frequently do not align with the knowledge and skills needed for postsecondary education. Students do not find out that they are unprepared for college until they are actually enrolled and find themselves struggling in credit-bearing courses, and huge proportions of students end up having to take remedial courses at great cost to themselves, their parents, or the state college system. This standards gap and lack of alignment do not exist in high-performing countries.

At the secondary level, most high-performing countries use curriculum-based external examinations that incorporate the country's overall standards into high-quality syllabi and examinations. These exams assess a major part of what students are expected to know and be able to do in all subjects, typically the language of instruction, mathematics, physics, biology, chemistry, earth sciences, geography, world history, their own country's history, economics, art, music, and foreign languages. Not every student takes every subject, but all are intentionally exposed to a broad curriculum. Good performance is judged against an external standard, not relative to other students in the school. These exams form clear gateways to the next stage of education or to careers, with which they are aligned. In terms of format, most use essay-type responses on timed examinations and also include some longer-term projects during the year. Some countries use oral examinations for parts of the subject.

There have been many studies of the impact of these curriculum-based examination systems. Across OECD, students in systems that require curriculum-based external examinations perform, on average, 16 points higher than those in school systems that do not use such examinations (OECD, 2011b). "The nations and provinces that use universal curriculum-based external exit exams (and often teacher grades as well) to signal student achievement have significantly higher achievement levels and smaller differentials by family background than otherwise comparable jurisdictions that base high-stakes decisions on voluntary college admissions tests and/or teacher grades" (Bishop, 2005, p. 27).

Why do these types of assessments inspire higher academic achievement? They are high-quality examinations designed by academic experts and the best teachers. The questions are published in the media after the examinations are over. They have greater credibility with parents than the kind of minimum-competency high school exit exams or accountability tests used in the United States. Examinations are graded externally, and, because they have no control over the exam, teachers are protected against the pressure to lower standards or raise grades.

The courses set high expectations, and students are motivated to study hard because the exams are a gateway to the next stage of education. Teacher training and professional development are also aligned with the examinations so that together they deliver a powerful, coherent system of instruction. We have considerable and growing experience with these kinds of tests with systems like the New York State Regents High School Examinations and the Advanced Placement (AP) and International Baccalaureate (IB) programs, but the latter two have only been taken by select groups of students rather than a whole cohort.

Critics of these external examination systems argue that there is too much memorization and teaching to the test. Also, where they are used as a single high-stakes gateway to the next step in the educational progression, as in China, for example, they cut off second-chance opportunities for students who may develop at a different pace. But they do not have to be set up that way. In Sweden, for example, the same examinations can be taken later in a student's school career.

There are, to be sure, many variations in how assessments are used internationally. Tests perform many functions in education— public accountability, informing and improving instructional practice, and monitoring student progress. No single assessment can satisfy all these purposes, and countries vary in how they balance these different demands. Finland, one of the highest-performing countries in the world on PISA assessments, uses primarily school-based assessments with only periodic sample testing from the national level to monitor quality. Singapore holds students accountable through examinations and holds teachers and principals accountable through a performance management system, but one that uses a wide variety of measures and inputs, not just student test scores. Most countries today share similar goals of raising achievement and reducing achievement gaps among groups, as well as the concomitant need for schools to be accountable for those results. But there is widespread concern about the negative effects on education systems of overweighting narrow external tests.

Both European and Asian countries are shifting the balance of their assessment systems toward greater use of formative assessment, better use of data by schools to improve instruction and performance, greater involvement of teachers in assessment, and more authentic measurement of higher-order skills. Linda Darling-Hammond (2010b) puts it this way:

> As a large and increasing part of their examination systems, high-achieving nations use open-ended performance tasks and school-based curriculum-embedded assessment to give students opportunities to develop and demonstrate higher-order thinking skills: the ability to find and organize information to solve problems, frame and conduct investigations, analyze and synthesize data, and apply learning to new situations. The curriculum and assessment systems evaluate students' abilities in projects, group work, open-ended tasks, and oral presentations as well as examinations that include essays and open-ended tasks and problems, along with summative tests using selected-response (multiple-choice) items usually given at the end of a course year. (p. 3)

This is a moment of great opportunity for schools in the United States. We desperately need a paradigm shift in assessment. The advent of the Common Core standards and the federal support for two large state consortia on assessment hold promise for focusing on teaching students more higher-order skills and assessing those skills in significantly better ways. The first round of new tests from the consortia are scheduled to be ready in 2014, although it will take a while for them to be integrated into classrooms on a wide scale. Getting assessment right will also take time, just as the previous kinds of tests took many years to perfect. We will also have to take into account competing priorities. Different stakeholders value different things: education policymakers want snapshot data at one point in time for management and accountability purposes, while education practitioners need instructionally valuable data. Assessments rarely collect both equally well. We are also still learning how to measure some of the new kinds of desired outcomes, such as creativity.

## Putting It All Together: Preparing Students for a Global Innovation Society

The ferment in the United States and internationally on curriculum and assessment are part and parcel of the changes in policies and strategies that countries are undertaking as they seek to move from good to great and adapt to the demands of a 21st century innovation economy. The United States has much to contribute to this international conversation in terms of our pedagogical practice and our research know-how, but we also have much to learn from other countries that achieve higher standards in literacy, math, and science for all or most of their students, while also inculcating global skills.

The development of the internationally benchmarked Common Core state standards is a major step in the direction of a world-class education, but the standards are not self-implementing. They will not magically transform education and raise achievement. They can sit on a shelf and be referred to by everyone but still have no bearing on teaching and learning in the classroom. High-performing countries have strong instructional systems in which standards are embedded in strong curricula, with logically organized learning progressions, matching authentic assessments, and both preservice teacher education and in-service professional development focused on this content. In the 1990s, when Massachusetts set high standards, organized substantial professional development around the standards, raised the entry bar for the teaching profession, and required that students meet the standards in order to graduate, its students' achievement increased significantly. Meanwhile, other states that had decent standards but did not put into place these other critical mechanisms showed little improvement in student achievement. We are all familiar with reform efforts that have been implemented weakly, lacking strong curricula or professional support for teachers. For the Common Core standards to lift Americans students' achievement to world-class levels, they will need to be accompanied by strong, content-rich curriculum, well-educated teachers using modern pedagogy, and better assessment.

As of today, Common Core standards have been developed only for reading and math, which could result in a further narrowing of the curriculum. High-performing countries are, if anything, broadening their curriculum. Countries that have focused heavily on science and math are adding or strengthening instruction in arts, health and physical education, global and environmental issues, languages, and soft skills like learning to learn and team building as part of a core curriculum for the 21st century. How do schools find the time to do all of this? The answer lies in focus. Strong systems have a broad but focused curriculum, centered on the most important concepts, not encyclopedic coverage.

Finally, the kinds of creativity, higher-order thinking, and self-management skills being called for to prepare students for the world of tomorrow put more emphasis on student-centered learning methods such as problem- and project-based learning. These methods are taught in pedagogy classes in schools of education, but even though teachers know about them and believe them to be effective, teachers tend not to use them much. Some advocates have contended that if teachers were just unleashed from all the accountability demands, they would naturally teach in a constructivist, learner-centered way. But teachers need help in this area, in the form of more robust training and curriculum guidance that deal with the high cognitive demands and potential classroom management issues of using student-centered methods. Changing practice in this direction will require an iterative process of planning, execution, and feedback.

The changes called for in this chapter are enormous, even daunting. Globalization is transforming our world in a way that is comparable in scale and disruption to the industrial revolution. Education-as-usual prepares our students for the world of yesterday, not the world of tomorrow. The good news is that we have strong examples of how to promote the new kind of teaching, learning, and assessment modeled all across the United States by effective schools, schools of education, and universities. Providing world-class educational opportunity for all our students will require districts and especially states to pull together all of the elements into an integrated whole.

**Reflection Questions**

Some of the policy changes necessary to support major change to curriculum, instruction, and assessment will have to be undertaken at the state and federal levels. Nevertheless, it is well worth considering what schools and communities can do while waiting for the Common Core standards and state assessment consortia to produce their work, and for broader innovations in curriculum and instruction to climb higher on the policy agenda. Here are some ideas to consider:

1. *World-class standards*: Examine with your school or district whether you are preparing all of your students for postsecondary education or advanced training, at least in terms of the Common Core standards in language arts and mathematics, which are available online at www.commoncore.org. What changes need to be made in your district's curriculum, instruction, teacher professional development, and student support to enable all students to reach these standards?

2. *Skills for global innovation societies:* Read major works on globalization, and engage fellow faculty members, administrators, parents, and students in reading and discussing these works. Can you say that your school curriculum is preparing students for the world of 2020 and beyond? Consider how your curriculum could add more inquiry-based approaches to science. Visit schools that have a strong focus on environmental sustainability or global literacy and languages. Explore how you can focus more strongly on higher-order thinking skills and problem solving in each subject area. Examine whether the learning environment in your school or district encourages open-ended curiosity, comfort with no right answers, creativity, and taking personal responsibility for identifying and solving problems. How can you focus your curriculum in order to address crucial new content areas?

3. *Modernizing assessment:* What options do you have when it comes to using assessments that balance standardized tests with greater use of performance assessments, like portfolios and exhibitions that emphasize higher-order cognitive skills development? How might you incorporate more rigorous curriculum-based assessment, like AP or IB exams, into your assessment practice? Consider benchmarking

yourselves directly against international peers by having students take publicly released PISA questions in science, math, or reading, download-able at www.pisa.oecd.org/dataoecd/47/23/41943106.pdf.

4. *Creating "rich tasks":* Review the "rich tasks" (projects) available for different age groups from the Queensland (Australia) Department of Education and Training's website (http://education.qld.gov.au/corporate/newbasics/html/richtasks/richtasks.html), together with the guide on how to create and score rich tasks (http://education.qld.gov.au/corporate/newbasics/html/richtasks/richtasks.html). How might these projects work with your students? How do you think they might react? Do they have the academic background to tackle the problems? Do they have the necessary problem-solving skills? If possible, try out a few of these projects with your students or create your own, and then reflect on the outcomes.

# 6

# CREATING THE FUTURE

The pace of change in our world is increasing exponentially. Economies have changed, societies have changed, and technology has changed. Only our schools remain recognizably similar to those of another era. We can't predict with any certainty what the jobs will be like in 20 years' time, but as educators, we owe it to our students to try to prepare them for this new and unpredictable world of tomorrow. We need all of our students to have the knowledge, skills, and dispositions to be able to compete, cooperate, and collaborate on a par with their peers around the world.

My purpose in writing this book is not to suggest that we should simply adopt the practices of the high-performing educational systems found in other countries. Culture matters. Context matters. We can't just copy and paste a practice from one system to another without adapting it to our own context. My goal is rather to provoke thought and to challenge some of our long-held beliefs about the way education "has to be" by looking at what countries that have been making significant progress over the past few decades have been doing while U.S. educational performance has remained flat. We can draw from our examination of the key drivers of other countries' progress as we seek to ensure that all U.S. students meet Common Core standards and, more broadly, are prepared for the 21st century.

Recognizing that education will be key to future economic growth and that low educational performance exacts significant economic costs, countries around the world are increasing graduation rates, raising achievement, making educational systems more equitable, and rethinking the skills needed for the 21st century global knowledge economy. A number of countries have made dramatic educational gains over the past two decades and are preparing to meet even greater challenges, as enormous countries like China and India provide education to more of their population. The systems we have looked at are not resting on their laurels, either. Alberta, a high-performing province in Canada, has been engaging its citizens in dialog about what an educated citizen should look like in 2039 (Alberta Ministry of Education, 2010). Singapore, another high-performing system, has conducted a visioning exercise as to what knowledge and skills, beliefs and attitudes, and social-emotional competencies young Singaporeans will need to be prepared for a global future (Singapore Ministry of Education, 2010).

Perhaps the most encouraging finding from international comparisons is that major improvement on a wide scale is possible within a few years, although the highest-performing countries keep at it for decades. The systems discussed in this book are diverse and use a different mix of strategies to suit their own contexts, but they do have some fundamental tenets in common, as discussed in Chapter 3. Once more, these are

- Vision and leadership
- Ambitious standards
- Commitment to equity
- High-quality teachers and leaders
- Alignment and coherence
- Management and accountability
- Student motivation
- Global and future orientation

The number of elements here reminds us that there are no silver bullets. Too often in our education debates, we seem to bounce from solution to solution; first establishing standards is the answer, then it's firing bad teachers, then changing assessment, then focusing on student engagement, then embracing charter schools, and so on. The United States, like many other countries, has implemented initiatives in many of these areas, but these initiatives will not move the needle toward high achievement on a broad and equitable scale until a combination of effective elements come together as a system. Because significant progress can take at least 5 to 10 years to be realized, success requires a clear sense of moral purpose, a guiding and persistent political coalition, effective leadership at many levels, a focus on building teachers' capacity in schools to carry out continuing improvements, engagement of broad support, the use of evidence to guide interventions, and a consistent orientation toward the future.

What knowledgeable international colleagues have told me when asked for their view of the American education system is that the United States is a tremendous innovator from which they have all learned a great deal. However, they observe—perhaps more clearly than we do ourselves—that the United States has failed to build an effective system of education to address the needs of *all* children. This is partly due to the inherent difficulties of achieving alignment when there are so many different levels of authority. Other perceived barriers are the universal acceptance of inequality in the structure and funding of schools, the lack of a human resource system for educator recruitment and development, and the frequency of policy changes without having built the capacity to implement those changes.

According to McKinsey studies of improving education systems (Barber & Mourshed, 2007), when educational systems have low and uneven achievement, strong government intervention is necessary. At the same time (to take a leaf out of the playbooks of successful corporations), you have to "unleash greatness." The more capable the teachers and school leaders, the less control is required from the center. The challenge to reform strategy in the United States is that we have large numbers of schools at many different levels of performance, so finding the right balance between mandates and autonomy is exceedingly tricky. Our mediocre performance on international assessments is substantially due to the low performance of our lowest-achieving students, but we don't have enough of our highest-achieving students performing at the highest levels either.

Education leaders' understanding of how important it is to look at what is happening in their field in other parts of the world has increased enormously in recent years. This has led to the development of internationally benchmarked Common Core standards in the United States, consortia to produce new kinds of assessments, and new conversation about how to recruit and develop a world-class teaching and leadership profession. While awareness of the critical need to improve our education system has grown, there isn't as yet a groundswell of support among the general public for a world-class education. States and districts have the power to change that reality through the following actions:

1. Engaging the public in envisioning what knowledge and skills our students will need to be successful as adults in 2030, 2040, and beyond.

2. Creating a broad leadership coalition across all sectors of education (K–12 and higher education, business, parents, students and community organizations) to benchmark against high-performing systems and steer a change agenda over five years.

3. Developing a strategy for identifying, recruiting, and supporting high-quality teachers and leaders and building instructional capacity in schools.

4. Designing and monitoring strategies to provide equity as a core part of the effort to provide world-class education.

It's important to remember that the G.I. Bill and the National Defense Education Act established the educational basis for U.S. leadership in the second half of the 20th century. When the Elementary and Secondary Education Act is reauthorized, it should have as its goal the development of a world-class preK–12 education system that embraces excellence, equity, and a global and future orientation.

## Technology and Innovation

Nothing stands still. The present does not predict the future. Just as people in the 1970s could not have imagined that Singapore, Finland, and Shanghai would one day outperform the United States educationally, so the strategies that have helped nations develop high-performing systems up until now may need to be modified for continued success (Segal, 2011). No one is more aware of this than the nations currently sitting atop the global scorecards. Countries like China are focused on shifting from quantity to quality in their education systems. Other countries are moving toward more personalized learning and away from a lockstep march through courses; toward a broader curriculum that emphasizes creativity and a global perspective; and toward changed roles for teachers and schools as information technology increasingly makes student-centered learning possible anytime, anywhere.

Technology has not been a major driver of educational improvement in high-performing countries up until now. In fact, a number of studies have concluded that the gigantic sums many governments have spent to equip schools with technology and provide ICT training have not had the positive effect on achievement that advocates predicted (Asia Society, 2010). Still, it is obvious that technology is changing every aspect of contemporary life, especially for young people. Technology's potential for helping U.S. schools address what international assessments have revealed to be serious educational challenges cannot be ignored. Consider the following advantages of technology:

• It enables students to take virtual courses on a wide variety of subjects even if there are no teachers who specialize in that subject in their schools. This is especially helpful in underresourced schools, whether rural or urban, or for simply exposing students to a broader, richer curriculum than is available in some local schools.

• It allows teachers to receive professional development from master teachers anytime, anywhere, and to form collaborative learning communities with other teachers in their fields even if the other teachers are not in their school or district.

- It expands learning time, freeing it from the limits of the traditional school day or school year.
- It facilitates the development of 21st century problem-solving and critical-thinking skills across a broad range of subjects of interest to students.
- It makes global classrooms and collaboration possible, allowing both teachers and students to expand their horizons.
- It allows students to conduct lab experiments online, even if their schools cannot provide regular lab equipment.
- It enables the highest-quality curriculum materials to be available to any school or child anywhere. For example, more than 8,000 university courses are now available free on the Internet for students and self-learners through open education resources (Smith, 2009).
- It enables assessment and feedback to be given in real time rather than days or even weeks later.
- It enables faster and more frequent communication between school and parents on the subjects of educational goals and progress.
- It allows instruction to be adapted to individual student needs. For example, student response systems allow teachers to adapt their teaching based on real-time evidence of student understanding. Instructional materials can be adapted to students who are behind, those who are ahead, or those who simply have different learning styles.
- It makes possible the development of powerful interactive simulations of complex phenomena as video gaming technology is combined with the findings of cognitive science.

In short, technology can provide enormous access for students and teachers and can significantly improve instructional practice, if properly deployed. Ironically, the transformative power of technology can probably be seen most clearly in countries that lack the standard infrastructure of schooling. For example, there are 15 million K–12 students taking online courses in Turkey (Patrick, 2010). In Brazil, classes are transmitted via videoconference to 25,000 students in 700 schools throughout the remote reaches of the Amazon jungle. The Open University in England has worked with a consortium of 15 universities in 9 African countries to provide in-service training to 250,000 teachers, many of whom have not received formal teacher preparation. A refugee camp in western Tanzania, an area with no electricity, was able to create a solar-powered computer center that brought learning content to students and adults alike in an area with no books or telephones. And researcher Sugata Mitra (2010) has been able to demonstrate through his "hole in the wall" experiments in Indian and Cambodian slums that uneducated children, working with peers, can use computers to learn without teacher guidance.

Perhaps because they are already succeeding through conventional means, high-performing countries have not yet seen transformative effects as a result of widespread incorporation of technology. However, they are all actively exploring how technology can take them to the next level. Korea, for example, has a national online tutoring system. Australia is creating nationwide, universal access to high-quality curriculum materials and making school data available to all parents through its national curriculum and MySchool web portals. China is using satellite technology to enable master teachers in cities to work with teachers in remote rural areas where vast distances make in-person professional development impractical. Singapore has moved through several phases of ICT integration: in the first phase, every single teacher received training in ICT; in the second phase, a number of school-based experiments on encouraging self-directed and collaborative learning were performed; and now, in Phase 3, these innovations are being spread throughout the system through regular professional development mechanisms for teachers and principals. Both Korea and Singapore are developing digital textbooks.

America is home to the creators of some of the world's most powerful digital tools, and we have wonderful examples of technological innovations, especially in the past 10 years, that could help with our challenges of unequal access, shortages of high-quality teachers, lack of student engagement, and access to high-quality curriculum. This is an area of strength that the United States can build on. It has to be said that most of these applications of technology have not been around long enough for their effectiveness to have been well researched, but as technologies develop to incorporate speech recognition, data mining, and artificial intelligence over the next decade, their potential to enhance educational practice will continue to grow.

Many people see technology's biggest promise as the ability to go beyond one-size-fits-all education to genuinely individualize learning and make it more student centered, as befits the 21st century learner who has grown up surrounded by technologies. This does not mean just letting students do what they want. (We all know that projects that are not in a larger curriculum framework of learning goals are just that—projects.) Instead, it means the teacher's role changes from transmitter of knowledge to one who guides and scaffolds student progress toward the achievement of broad, deep, and ambitious learning goals. While some may find this vision of schooling far-fetched, it is often the edges of a business that reshape the business (Chen, 2010). And budget crises and teacher shortages may well facilitate the progress of this "disruptive innovation" (Christensen, Horn, & Johnson, 2008).

However, getting personalized and effective learning at scale is not just a matter of exploiting the strengths of the technology. If our efforts do not sit within a system that has ambitious standards, a commitment to equity, and a human resource system that recruits and supports teachers who can combine deep content and diagnostic knowledge with the ability to use digital technology, then we will have more pockets of excellence (this time digital), but continued weak results on international assessments.

## A New Worldview: Learning How to Learn

How can we ensure that we do not become antiquated and insular, and that we are positioned for the continuous improvement that the modern world will demand? We can't predict the changes that globalization and technology will require of us. Taking our cue from Einstein, who famously said that "everything has changed except the way we think," we need to find mechanisms to keep ourselves outward and future oriented. People and ideas now traverse the globe with unprecedented speed and frequency. Internationalization affects every field of our endeavor. Yet American education has not been systematically informed by the experience of other countries. We can no more afford to isolate ourselves educationally than we can economically or in terms of national security.

How can we strengthen our ability to learn from the experiences of other countries and make those lessons more effective in our own contexts? Currently, most educators and parents know little more about education in other countries than that we are not number one in math and science. There are myriad lessons to be learned from international comparisons, but it takes time to learn enough about other systems to understand the interconnectedness of structures and practices. International exchanges—of information and people—can help us understand and tailor the experiences of others to our own situation. Moreover, such cross-cultural interaction can help education leaders to comprehend the competition that our students will be facing in future years and prepare our students for their citizenship roles in an interconnected world. If we are to thrive in this global age, we must make a serious commitment to establishing mechanisms that promote international learning (Kagan & Stewart, 2005). Here are some suggestions.

## Broaden and Deepen the Range of Research

Large-scale international surveys of student achievement have been the most widely visible aspect of comparative research. They have provided us some key common indicators and ignited a critical discussion of excellence, equity, and productivity. But we also need more in-depth studies of high-priority issues across a range of countries. For example, we know that high-performing systems produce higher achievement at lower cost than the United States, so what is different about the ways in which they allocate their education resources? What models of vocational education and workforce skills training are most effective in the 21st century? What forms of intervention, in elementary, secondary, and higher education, have the greatest effect on dropout rates? Studies that focus on questions like these will give policymakers and practitioners a wider set of thoroughly examined options and convey some sense of the trade-offs necessary so that they can consider them seriously.

Joint research projects are increasingly common in science, health, and industry, but they are rare in education. Such projects looking into high-priority topics of mutual interest would be valuable.

## Involve States and Cities in International Benchmarking

The United States is the only federal system that does not draw state samples on international assessments like PISA. Therefore, even though individual U.S. states vary enormously in their achievement levels, they cannot directly compare their results with those in high-performing systems. They can only use a national average for comparison. With federal assistance, interested states should participate in the next round of PISA assessments in reading, math, and science so that they can benchmark themselves internationally. Some states might also want to follow Ohio's lead by inviting an audit of their policies and practices to see how they compare with the best in the world and identify key areas for improvement (Achieve, 2007). And cities and districts are the nexus where policy and practice come together for students. By sharing challenges with systems where education is improving, cities might also glean useful ideas for innovation.

## Involve Practitioners in International Dialogue

Learning from the world also needs to move beyond the realm of academic researchers and international organizations to involve practitioners. Just as in countries like Finland, China, and Singapore, where these processes have a stronger hold, teachers and school leaders could be involved in the formulation and conduct of all sorts of exchanges. Given the importance of teacher quality to excellence in education, there is no reason why outstanding teachers could not be involved in observing classroom practices in other countries. Outstanding principals could take part in short-term shadowing of their peers in countries where there are practices of interest to the United States. Information technologies also allow teachers or principals to communicate regularly with their peers in another country, comparing teaching units and the quality of student work. Such globally minded faculty will be needed to help prepare globally competent students.

## Create International Partnerships

Beyond short-term international exchanges and studies, institutional partnerships of various kinds provide opportunities for more in-depth understanding of other countries, cultures, and systems as well as different aspects of educational practice. Just as no business can be successful today without understanding business practices around the world, so our teachers and school and state leaders need to understand how to incorporate an international dimension into education and be able to compare our educational system against international benchmarks. In many parts of higher education, such internationalization is well underway, but there are relatively few international partnerships concerned with K–12 education.

Institutional partnerships between states, schools, and colleges of education in different countries would, for example, encourage prospective teachers to understand the international dimensions of their subject so that they could incorporate international content and perspective into their teaching (Longview Foundation, 2008). Aspiring principals could examine different ideas about effective school practice. International partnerships could build capacity on both sides and foster a generation of more globally savvy educators and students. At Asia Society, we have been involved in helping schools create school-to-school partnerships, especially with schools in China. These can start off in a small way, with brief exchanges, and progress toward regular structured activities for students, teachers, and school leaders, both in person and online (see Figure 7). They can foster language learning and cultural understanding (Asia Society, 2006a), teach students how to work in global teams, and facilitate the exploration of global issues.

No nation has a patent on excellence. Like the children we serve, we are all learners. The immediate challenge, therefore, is to create learning environments through which educators can learn from and with the

| Figure 7 | Partnership Development Matrix for Interactions with Chinese Schools | | |
|---|---|---|---|
| **Partnership Arrangement** | **Students** | **Faculty** | **Leaders** |
| **Basic** | Engage in brief exchange activities that require little or no Chinese language competency.<br><br>**Via Technology**<br>• Introductory videoconferencing<br>• Join a group online community with students in China<br><br>**In Person**<br>• Short trip to experience China | Establish initial contact with partner school.<br><br>**Via Technology**<br>• Establish e-mail connection with teachers in China<br>• Join online community<br><br>**In Person**<br>• Participate in a short-term study mission<br>• Host short-term visiting teachers from China | Investigate a partnership.<br><br>**Via Technology**<br>• Establish e-mail connection with principals in China<br>• Join online community<br><br>**In Person**<br>• Engage in initial contact with the partner school through mutual visit<br>• Participate in some communication with key contacts in the partner school |
| **Intermediate** | Participate in short-term, well-structured projects with emphasis on language learning.<br><br>**Via Technology**<br>• Share media or laboratory projects with students in China<br><br>**In Person**<br>• Summer camp<br>• Visits with home stay | Maintain regular contact with partner school teachers via online or in-person activities.<br><br>**Via Technology**<br>• Post instructional materials<br>• Study and adapt materials posted by Chinese teachers<br><br>**In Person**<br>• Classroom shadowing<br>• Joint professional training<br>• Engage colleagues in other disciplines | Conduct regular/ in-depth partnership activities with partner school leaders.<br><br>**Via Technology**<br>• Establish a school-to-school portal web page that facilitates programs and activities<br><br>**In Person**<br>• Participate in regular communication with the partner school<br>• Host a principal shadow group from China<br>• Organize community events |

*continued*

| Figure 7 | Partnership Development Matrix for Interactions with Chinese Schools (continued) | | |
|---|---|---|---|
| Partnership Arrangement | Students | Faculty | Leaders |
| Advanced | Regularly participate in longer-term collaborative programs that connect with the curriculum. | Conceptualize and organize activities that regularly connect the school's teachers and students. | Organize and participate in regular structured partnership activities. |
| | **Via Technology**<br>• Identify, research, and propose solutions to a shared problem through online collaboration<br>• Debate on relevant topics | **Via Technology**<br>• Creatively use technology to conduct joint units or for project instruction | **Via Technology**<br>• Explore new technologies/resources to enhance school-to-school partnership overall |
| | **In Person**<br>• Joint projects<br>• Joint seminars and discussions<br>• In-session visits<br>• Community service | **In Person**<br>• Exchange curriculum<br>• Co-direct a project for a specific unit<br>• Organize a seminar on a topic of mutual interest | **In Person**<br>• Joint training with counterpart principals<br>• Engage the community in convening resources for furthering of the partnership |

*Source:* From *US-China Partnership Development Matrix* (p. 4) by Jeff Wang. Copyright 2011 by Asia Society. Available online at http://asiasociety.org/files/exchange-matrix.pdf. Adapted with permission.

world. Historically, U.S. education has been influenced by ideas from around the world, but these influences have been episodic. Today, modern travel and communication technology make global connection easier, but only a relatively small group of people have as yet had the opportunity to take advantage of those connections. Nevertheless, as education innovations are taking hold across the planet and international exchange is fueling new thinking, we can accelerate the improvement of our own education system by examining those in other nations. While the United States has a lot to learn, it also has an important role to play in improving education around the world. It is time to adopt a new worldview, be open to others' practice, and be willing to share our own experiences as we seek to educate all our children for this new global era.

American schools hold a society of the future, creating the young adults who will take over from us in a few years' time. We need our graduates to be the best they can be, so we must give them the knowledge and skills to take part in an innovation society with a more global perspective. The United States is still seen as a world leader in science, technology, and innovation. If we combine our existing strengths with learning from the world to find ways to achieve excellence and equity at scale, we can truly provide a world-class education for our children and grandchildren.

# ACKNOWLEDGMENTS

There are marvelous teachers everywhere. Over the course of my career, I have been fortunate to meet and learn from many remarkable individuals, who have opened the world to me. They include teachers, principals, and community leaders in schools in Africa, western and eastern Europe, North America, and many parts of Asia, who have generously shared with me their challenges and accomplishments. They are too numerous to mention by name, but this book could not have been written without them.

At university, my dissertation supervisor, sociologist A. H. (Chelly) Halsey, whose seminal research had helped to reform the highly elitist educational system in England, encouraged me to think about the big factors that shape educational achievement and encouraged my interest in understanding these factors in an international and comparative context.

After moving to New York, I was privileged to work for many years at Carnegie Corporation with a wonderful group of colleagues, board members, and grantees. Under admired presidents Alan Pifer, David Hamburg, and Vartan Gregorian, I had the opportunity to collaborate with innovators and reformers from all over the United States, including early childhood development leaders such as Lynne Kagan; advocates for the teaching profession such as Linda Darling-Hammond and Jim

Kelly; policy leaders such as governors James B. Hunt Jr., Richard Riley, and Tom Kean; and pioneers in providing social supports outside school such as Jim Comer and Jane Quinn. I learned a great deal from all of them and owe them an immense debt of gratitude.

After Carnegie, my career became more international and took me next to the United Nations. I am especially grateful to Sadako Ogata, then UN High Commissioner for Refugees, and to Olara Otunu, then Special Representative of the Secretary General for Children and Armed Conflict, for the opportunity to work on Initiatives to expand access to schools for children in the most dire circumstances.

Finally, as vice president of Asia Society under the leadership of its visionary president, Vishakha Desai, I have had the opportunity to witness the rise of Asia and to see firsthand the rapid pace of globalization and the acceleration of excellence and equity in educational systems in many parts of the world. At Asia Society, I have worked with and am grateful to a close group of education colleagues, led by Tony Jackson, Michael Levine, and Shuhan Wang, with whom I share the conviction that the United States needs a more fundamental response to the educational challenges of globalization and must be open to the experiences of high-performing and rapidly improving education systems.

This book is based on my accumulated experiences over many years. But during the writing of the book, I benefited particularly from conversations with Andreas Schleicher of OECD; Marc Tucker of the National Center on Education and the Economy; Lee Sing Kong of the National Institute of Education in Singapore; Pasi Sahlberg of the Ministry of Education in Finland; Brian McGaw of the University of Melbourne; Michelle Cahill of Carnegie Corporation; Minxuan Zhang of Shanghai University; Susan Sclafani of the Pearson Foundation; Yong Zhao of Oregon University; Fernando Reimers of Harvard University; Linda Darling-Hammond of Stanford University; Kai-ming Cheng of the University of Hong Kong; and policy colleagues in ministries of education in many countries.

At ASCD, I would particularly like to thank Executive Director Gene Carter, whose leadership is making the organization more deeply international; Genny Ostertag, acquisitions editor, who encouraged my interest in pulling together what I had learned from my experiences in the United States and internationally; and Katie Martin, senior editor, whose editing has always been positive and helpful and has made the book substantially clearer.

The motivation and primary support for this book come from my family. My deepest thanks and appreciation go to my husband, Michael, and to our children, Emma, Abigail, and Justin, and their spouses, Richard, Matthew, and Dree, for their encouragement, their probing questions, and their own lively engagement with the world of the 21st century. This book is dedicated to them and to my grandson, Nathaniel (and any others who may follow!), in the hope that it will contribute to the urgent debate as to how the United States can provide a world-class education to all of our children and grandchildren.

# REFERENCES

Achieve, Inc. (2007). *Creating a world-class education system in Ohio.* Washington, DC: Author. Available: http://www.achieve.org/files/World_Class_Edu_Ohio_FINAL.pdf

Achieve, Inc. (2010). *What states should know about international standards in science: Highlights from Achieve's analysis.* Available: http://www.achieve.org/filesWHATSTATESHOULDKNOWABOUTINTERNATIONALSTANDARDSINSCIENCE.pdf

ACT. (2011). *Affirming the goal: Is college and career readiness an internationally competitive standard?* Iowa City, IA: Author.

Adams, K. (2005). *The sources of innovation and creativity.* Paper commissioned by the National Center on Education and the Economy for the New Commission on the Skills of the American Workforce. Washington, DC: National Center on Education and the Economy.

Alberta Initiative for School Improvement (AISI). (n.d.). Home page. Retrieved November 3, 2011, from http://education.alberta.ca/department/ipr/aisi.aspx

Alberta Ministry of Education. (2010). *Inspiring education: A dialogue with Albertans* Available: https://www.inspiringeducation.alberta.ca

Alberts, B. (2009). Restoring science to science education. *Carnegie Reporter.* New York: Carnegie Corporation of New York.

Alliance for Excellent Education. (2009, August). The high cost of high school dropouts: What the nation pays for inadequate high schools. *Issue Brief.* Washington, DC: Author. Available: http://www.all4ed.org/files/HighCost.pdf

Alliance for Excellent Education. (2011, May). A time for deeper learning: Preparing students for a changing world. *Policy Brief.* Washington, DC: Author. Available: http://www.all4ed.org/files/DeeperLearning.pdf

American Council on the Teaching of Foreign Languages (ACTFL). (2010). *National enrollment survey preliminary result.* Alexandria, VA: Author.

American Council on the Teaching of Foreign Languages (ACTFL). (2011). *Foreign language enrollment in K–12 public schools: Are students ready for a global society?* Alexandria, VA: Author.

Asia Society. (2006a). *Creating a Chinese language program in your school.* New York. Author.

Asia Society. (2006b). *Math and science education in a global age: What the U.S. can learn from China.* New York: Author.

Asia Society. (2008a). *Going global: Preparing our students for an interconnected world.* New York: Author.

Asia Society. (2008b). *New skills for a global innovation society: Asia-Pacific Leaders Forum on Secondary Education, India.* New York: Author.

Asia Society. (2010). *Meeting the challenge: Preparing Chinese language teachers for American schools.* New York: Author.

Asia Society. (2011). *Improving teacher quality around the world: The International Summit on the Teaching Profession.* New York: Author.

Asia Society & Council of Chief State School Officers. (2010). *International perspectives on U.S. policy and practice: What can we learn from high-performing nations?* Available: http://asiasociety.org/files/pdf/learningwiththeworld.pdf

Australian Curriculum, Assessment, and Reporting Authority (ACARA). (2011). *Australian curriculum.* Available: http://www.acara.edu.au/curriculum/curriculum.html

Australian Institute for Teaching and School Leadership (AITSL). (n.d.). Home page. Retrieved November 3, 2011, from http://www.aitsl.edu.au/

Barber, M., & Mourshed, M. (2007). *How the world's best-performing school systems come out on top.* Available: http://www.mckinsey.com/App_Media/Reports/SSO/Worlds_School_Systems_Final.pdf

Barber, M., Whelan, F., & Clark, M. (2010, November). *Capturing the leadership premium: How the world's top school systems are building leadership capacity for the future.* London: McKinsey. Available: http://mckinseyonsociety.com/capturing-the-leadership-premium/

Bishop, J. H. (2005). *High school exit examinations: When do learning effects generalize?* (CAHRS Working Paper #05-04). Ithaca, NY: Cornell University, School of Industrial and Labor Relations, Center for Advanced Human Resource Studies. Available: DigitalCommons.ILR.cornell.edu/cahrswp/4

Boix-Mansilla, V., & Jackson, A. (2011). *Educating for global competence: Preparing our youth to engage the world.* New York: Asia Society; and Washington, DC: Council of Chief State School Officers.

Carmichael, S. B., Wilson, W. S., Finn, C. E., Jr., Winkler, A. M., & Palmieri, S. (2009). *Stars by which to navigate? Scanning national and international education standards in 2009.* Washington, DC: Thomas B. Fordham Foundation & Institute. Available: http://www.edexcellencemedia.net/publications/2009/200910_ starsbywhichtonavigate/Stars%20by%20Which%20to%20Navigate%20-%20 October%202009.pdf

Chen, M. (2010). *Education nation: Six leading edges of innovation in our schools.* San Francisco: Jossey-Bass.

Cheng, K. (2010). China: Turning the bad master into a good servant. In I. C. Rotberg (Ed.), *Balancing change and tradition in global education reform* (pp. 3–14). Lanham, MD: Rowan & Littlefield Education.

Chinese Ministry of Education. (2010). *National outline for medium- and long-term education reform and development.* Available:http://www.moe.edu.cn/ publicfiles/business/htmlfiles/moe/s3501/index.html

Christensen, C. M., Horn, M. B., & Johnson, C. W. (2008). *Disrupting class: How disruptive innovation will change the way the world learns.* New York: McGraw-Hill.

Cloud, J. P. (2010). *Educating for a sustainable future.* In H. H. Jacobs (Ed)., *Curriculum 21: Essential education for a changing world* (pp. 168–185). Alexandria, VA: ASCD.

Committee for Economic Development. (2006). *Education for global leadership: The importance of international studies and foreign language education for U.S. economic and national security.* Washington, DC: Author. Available: http:// www.ced.org/images/library/reports/education/report_foreignlanguages.pdf

Compton, R. A. (Executive Producer), Raney, A. (Producer), & Heeter, C. (Producer/ Director). (2009). *2 million minutes* [Film]. True South Studios LLC.

Conference Board. (2006). *Are they really ready to work?* Available: www.conference-board.org/topics/publicationdetail.cfm?publicationsid=1218

Darling-Hammond, L. (2010a). *The flat world and education: How America's commitment to equity will determine our future.* New York: Teachers College Press.

Darling-Hammond, L. (2010b). *Performance counts: Assessment systems that support high-quality learning.* Washington, DC: Council of Chief State School Officers. Available: http://flareassessment.org/resources/Paper_Assessment_ DarlingHammond.pdf

Darling-Hammond, L., & Rothman, R. (Eds.). (2011). *Teacher and leader effectiveness in high-performing education systems.* Washington, DC: Alliance for Excellent Education; and Stanford, CA: Center for Opportunity Policy in Education. Available: http://www.all4ed.org/files/TeacherLeaderEffectivenessReport.pdf

Day, M. (2011, June). *TDA approaches to improving teacher training.* Presentation at the OECD–Japan Seminar, Tokyo.

Fandel, L L. (2008, December 7). Alberta keeps pushing to improve its schools. *Des Moines Register*. Available: http://www.desmoinesregister.com/ article/20081207/OPINION01/812070309/Alberta-keeps-pushing-improve -its-schools

Federico, C., & Cloud, J. (2009). Kindergarten through twelfth grade education: Fragmentary progress in equipping students to think and act in a challenging world. In J. Dornbuch (Ed.), *Agenda for a sustainable America* (pp. 109–127). Washington, DC: ELI Press, Environmental Law Institute.

Friedman, T. L. (2005). *The world is flat: A brief history of the twenty-first century*. New York: Farrar, Straus and Giroux.

Fuchs, T., & Woessmann, L. (2004). *What accounts for international differences in student performance? A re-examination using PISA data*. CESifo Working Paper 1235. Available: http://www.cesifo-group.de/portal/pls/portal/ docs/1/1189152.PDF

Fullan, M. (2001). *The new meaning of educational change*. New York: Teachers College Press.

Ginsburg, A., Cooke, G., Leinwand, S., Noell, J., & Pollock, E. (2005). *Reassessing U.S. international mathematics performance: New findings from the 2003 TIMSS and PISA*. Washington, DC: American Institutes for Research. Available: http:// www.air.org/files/TIMSS_PISA_math_study1.pdf

Ginsburg, A., Leinwand, S., Anstrom, T., & Pollock, E. (2005). *What the United States can learn from Singapore's world-class mathematics system: An exploratory study*. Washington, DC: American Institutes for Research. Available: http:// www.air.org/files/Singapore_Report_Bookmark_Version1.pdf

Gladwell, M. (2008). *Outliers: The story of success*. New York: Little, Brown.

Goh, K. S. (1979). *Report on the Ministry of Education 1978*. Singapore: Singapore National Printers.

Goslin, D. A. (2003). *Engaging minds: Motivation and learning in America's schools*. Lanham, MD: Scarecrow Press.

Grubb, W. N. (2007, October). Dynamic inequality and intervention: Lessons from a small country. *Phi Delta Kappan, 89*(2), 105–114.

Hamburg, D. A. (1992). *Today's children: Creating a future for a generation in crisis*. New York: Random House.

Hargreaves, A., Halasz, G., & Pont, B. (2007). *School leadership for systemic improvement in Finland. A case study*. Paris: OECD. Available: http://www.oecd.org/ dataoecd/43/17/39928629.pdf

Hong, K. T., Mei, Y. S., & Lim, J. (2009). *The Singapore model method for learning mathematics*. Singapore: EPB Pan Pacific.

Hopkins, D. (2007). *Every school a great school: Realizing the potential of system leadership*. Maidenhead, UK: Open University Press.

Hoskins, B., & Fedriksson, U. (2008). *Learning to learn: What is it and can it be measured?* Luxembourg: Office for Official Publications of the European Communities. Available: http://publications.jrc.ec.europa.eu/repository/handle/111111111/979

Iswaran, S. (2011, March 16). Remarks presented at the International Summit on the Teaching Profession, New York, NY.

Jacobs, H. H. (Ed.). (2010). *Curriculum 21: Essential education for a changing world.* Alexandria, VA: ASCD.

James B. Hunt Jr. Institute for Educational Leadership and Policy. (2011). Higher ed and the common core standards. *Issue Brief.* Chapel Hill, NC: Author.

Jerald, C. D. (2009). *Defining a 21st century education.* Alexandria, VA: Center for Public Education. Available: http://www.centerforpubliceducation.org/Main-Menu/Policies/21st-Century-Education-Full-report-PDF.pdf

Kagan, S. L., & Stewart, V. (2005). A new world view: Education in a global era. *Phi Delta Kappan, 87*(3), 241–245.

Lee, S. K., Goh, C. B., Fredriksen, B., & Tan, J. P. (Eds.). (2008). *Toward a better future: Education and training for economic development in Singapore since 1965.* Washington, DC: World Bank.

Levin, B. (2008). *How to change 5000 schools: A practical and positive approach for leading change at every level.* Cambridge, MA: Harvard Education Press.

Levin, B., Glaze, A., & Fullan, M. (2008). Results without rancor or ranking: Ontario's success story. *Phi Delta Kappan, 90*(4), 273–280.

Levy, F., & Murnane, R. J. (2004). *The new division of labor: How computers are creating the next job market.* Princeton, NJ: Princeton University Press.

Longview Foundation. (2008). *Teacher preparation for the global age: The imperative for change.* Available: http://www.longviewfdn.org/files/44.pdf

McGaw, B. (2010). President's report: Transforming school education. *Dialogue, 29*(1). Available: www.assa.edu.au/publications/dialogue/2010_Vol29_No1.php

McKinsey. (2011, January). *What happens next? Five crucibles of innovation shaping the coming decade.* Presentation to Asia Society, New York.

McKinsey Global Institute. (2009). *Averting the next energy crisis: The demand challenge.* Available: www.mckinsey.com/mgi/reports/pdfs/next_energy

Mitra, S. (2010, July). *The child-driven education.* Available: http://www.ted.com/talks/lang/eng/sugata_mitra_the_child_driven_education.html

National Academy of Sciences. (2005). *Rising above the gathering storm: Energizing and employing America for a brighter economic future.* Report from the Committee on Prospering in the Global Economy of the 21st Century and Committee on Science, Engineering, and Public Policy. Washington, DC: National Academies Press.

National Academy of Sciences. (2007). *Taking science to school: Learning and teaching science in grades K–8.* Report from the Committee on Science Learning in K through Eighth Grade. Washington, DC: National Academies Press.

National Assessment of Educational Progress. (2011). *The nation's report card: Geography 2010.* Washington, DC: Author. Available: www.nationsreportcard.gov

National Center for Public Policy and Higher Education. (2008). *Measuring up 2008: The national report card on higher education.* Available: http://measuringup2008.highereducation.org/

National Center on Education and the Economy. (2007). *Tough choices or tough times: The report of the New Commission on the Skills of the American Workforce.* San Francisco: Wiley.

National Commission on Excellence in Education. (1983). *A nation at risk: The imperative for educational reform: A report to the Nation and the Secretary of Education, United States Department of Education.* Washington, DC: Author.

National Governors Association, Council of Chief State School Officers, & Achieve, Inc. (2008). *Benchmarking for success: Ensuring U.S. students receive a world-class education.* Available: http://www.achieve.org/files/BenchmarkingforSuccess.pdf

National Institute of Education. (2009). *TE21: A teacher education model for the 21st century.* Singapore: Author. Available: http://www.nie.edu.sg/files/about-nie/TE21%20online%20version.pdf

National Knowledge Commission. (2009). *Final report.* Delhi: Author. Available at http://www.knowledgecommission.gov.in

National Research Council. (2007). *International education and foreign languages: Keys to securing America's future.* Report of the Committee to Review the Title VI and Fulbright-Hays International Education Programs. Washington, DC: National Academies Press.

National Research Council. (2011). *A framework for K–12 science education: Practices, crosscutting concepts, and core ideas.* Available: http://www.nap.edu/catalog.php?record_id=13165

Ng, P. T. (2008a). Developing forward-looking and innovative school leaders: The Singapore Leaders in Education Programme. *Journal of In-service Education, 34*(2), 237–255.

Ng, P. T. (2008b). Educational reform in Singapore: From quantity to quality. *Educational Research for Policy and Practice, 7*(1), 5–15.

Oakes, J. (2005). *Keeping track: How schools structure inequality.* New Haven, CT: Yale University Press.

Obama, B. (2009, March 10). Remarks of the president of the United States to the Hispanic Chamber of Commerce.

Office for Standards in Education, Children's Services and Skills (Ofsted). (2010, September 10). *Finnish pupils' success in mathematics* (Report No. 100105). Available: http://www.ofsted.gov.uk/resources/finnish-pupils-success-mathematics

Organisation for Economic Co-operation and Development (OECD). (2008). *Improving school leadership*. Available: http://www.oecd.org/edu/schoolleadership

Organisation for Economic Co-operation and Development (OECD). (2009). *Education at a glance 2008: OECD indicators*. Paris: OECD Publications.

Organisation for Economic Co-operation and Development (OECD). (2010a). *The high cost of low educational performance: The long-run economic impact of improving PISA outcomes*. Available: http://www.oecd.org/data oecd/11/28/44417824.pdf

Organisation for Economic Co-operation and Development (OECD). (2010b). *PISA 2009 results: Executive summary*. Available: http://www.oecd.org/data oecd/34/60/46619703.pdf

Organisation for Economic Co-operation and Development (OECD). (2011a). *Building a high-quality teaching profession: Lessons from around the world*. Background report for the International Summit on the Teaching Profession. Available: http://www2.ed.gov/about/inits/ed/internationaled/background.pdf

Organisation for Economic Co-operation and Development (OECD). (2011b). *Lessons from PISA for the United States: Strong performers and successful reformers in education*. Paris: OECD Publications.

O'Toole, J., & Lawler, E. E. (2006). *The new American workplace*. New York: Palgrave Macmillan.

Partnership for 21st Century Skills. (2009). *Framework for 21st century learning*. Tucson, AZ: Partnership for 21st Century Skills. Available: http://www.p21.org/documents/P21_Framework.pdf

Patrick, S. (2010, November 16). *The online learning imperative*. Presentation to the 2010 Virtual School Symposium, Glendale, Arizona.

Pervin, B., & Campbell, C. (2011). Systems for teacher and leader effectiveness and quality: Ontario, Canada. In L. Darling-Hammond & R. Rothman (Eds.), *Teacher and leader effectiveness in high-performing systems* (pp. 23–33). Washington, DC: Alliance for Excellent Education; and Stanford, CA: Center for Opportunity Policy in Education.

Quek, G., et al. (Eds.). (2008). *TIMSS 2007 encyclopedia: A guide to mathematics and science education around the world*. Chestnut Hill, MA: TIMSS & PIRLS International Study Center, Boston College.

Reimers, F. (2009, September). Leading for global competency. *Educational Leadership, 67*(1) [online only]. Available: http://www.ascd.org/publications/educational-leadership/sept09/vol67/num01/Leading-for-Global-Competency.aspx

Rhodes, N. C., & Pufahl, I. (2009). *Foreign language teaching in U.S. schools: Results of a national survey*. Washington, DC: Center for Applied Linguistics.

Rotherham, A. J., & Willingham, D. (2009, September). 21st century skills: The challenges ahead. *Educational Leadership, 87*(1), 16–21.

Rouse, C. E. (2005, October). *The labor market consequences of inadequate education.* Paper prepared for the Symposium on the Social Costs of Inadequate Education, Teachers College, Columbia University, New York.

Sahlberg, P. (2011). *Finnish lessons: What can the world learn from educational change in Finland?* New York: Teachers College Press.

Schleicher, A. (2007, October 4). *Seeing U.S. education through the prism of international comparison.* Presentation at a meeting of the Alliance for Excellence in Education, Washington, DC.

Schleicher, A., & Stewart, V. (2008). Learning from world-class schools. *Educational Leadership, 66*(2), 44–51.

Schmidt, W. (2005). The role of curriculum. *American Educator, 23*(4). Available: http://www.aft.org/newspubs/periodicals/ae/fall2005/schmidt.cfm

Schmidt, W. (2008, June 9). Comments at the Hunt Institute and National Governors Association Governors Education Symposium, Cary, North Carolina.

Schmidt, W. H., Houang, R., & Shakrani, S. (2009). *International lessons about national standards.* Washington, DC: Thomas Fordham Institute.

Schwab, K. (Ed.). (2010). *The global competitiveness report 2010–2011.* Geneva: World Economic Forum.

Sclafani, S. (2008). *Rethinking human capital in education: Singapore as a model for teacher development.* Washington, DC: Aspen Institute. Available: http://www.aspeninstitute.org/sites/default/files/content/docs/education%20and%20society%20program/SingaporeEDU.pdf

Segal, A. (2011). *Advantage: How American innovation can overcome the Asian challenge.* New York: Norton.

Singapore Ministry of Education. (2010). *Nurturing our young for the future: Competencies for the 21st century.* Available: www.moe.gov.sg/committee-of-supply-debate/files/nurturing-our-young.pdf

Smith, M. S. (2009). Opening education. *Science, 323*(5910), 89–93.

Stevenson, H. W., & Stigler, J. W. (2006). *The learning gap: Why our schools are failing and what we can learn from Japanese and Chinese education* (2nd ed.). New York: Simon and Schuster.

Stewart, V. (2007, April). Becoming citizens of the world. *Educational Leadership, 64*(7), 8–14.

Stewart, V. (2010). A classroom as wide as the world. In H. H. Jacobs (Ed.), *Curriculum 21: Essential education for a changing world* (pp. 97–114). Alexandria, VA: ASCD.

Stewart, V. (2010/2011, December/January). Raising teacher quality around the world. *Educational Leadership, 68*(4), 16–20.

Stewart, V. (2011a, June). *Comparing East Asian and Western education systems: What sets them apart and what can they learn from each other.* Presentation at the OECD–Japan Seminar, Tokyo.

Stewart, V. (2011b). Singapore: Rapid improvement followed by strong performance. In OECD, *Lessons from PISA for the United States: Strong performers and successful reformers in education* (pp. 159–175). Paris: OECD Publications.

Stewart, V., & Singmaster, H. (2010, December 13). Lifting standards for all: China and the US can teach each other about education. *South China Morning Post.*

Stigler, J. W., & Hiebert, J. (1999). *The teaching gap: Best ideas from the world's teachers for improving education in the classroom.* New York: Free Press.

Tierney, T. J. (2006, May). How is American higher education measuring up? An outsider's perspective. In J. B. Hunt Jr. & T. J. Tierney, *American higher education: How does it measure up for the 21st Century?* (pp. 7–12) (National Center Report No. 06-2). San Jose, CA: National Center for Public Policy and Higher Education. Available: http://www.highereducation.org/reports/hunt_tierney/Hunt_Tierney.pdf

Torney-Purta, J., Lehmann, R., Oswald, H., & Schulz, W. (2001). *Citizenship and education in twenty-eight countries: Civic knowledge and engagement at age 14.* Amsterdam: International Association for the Evaluation of Educational Achievement.

Tucker, M (2011). *Standing on the shoulders of giants: An American agenda for education reform.* Washington, DC: National Center on Education and the Economy.

Uh, S. (2008). *How did Korea achieve the highest secondary education rate in the world?* Paper presented at meeting of Asia Society, New Delhi, India.

UNESCO. (2010). *Education for All global monitoring report: Reaching the marginalized.* Paris: UNESCO; and Oxford, UK: Oxford University Press.

U.S. Bureau of Labor Statistics. (2009). Table A-4: Employment status of the civilian population 25 years and over by educational attainment. Washington, DC: U.S. Department of Labor. Available: http://www.bls.gov/news.release/empsit.t04.htm

U.S. Census Bureau. (2004). Table 2: Exports from manufacturing establishments. Washington, DC: U.S. Department of Commerce.

U.S. Census Bureau. (2006). Table 8: Income in 2005 by educational attainment of the population 18 years and over. Washington, DC: U.S. Department of Commerce.

U.S. Census Bureau. (2008, August 14). *An older and more diverse nation by mid-century.* Available: http://www.census.gov/newsroom/releases/archives/population/cb08-123.html

Utah Department of Education. (2011). *Utah's dual immersion programs.* Available: www.schools.utah.gov/CURR/dualimmersion

Varmus, H. (2009, November 5). Remarks at the City of New York and Alfred P. Sloan Foundation First Annual Awards for Excellence in Teaching Science and Mathematics, New York.

Wagner, T. (2008). *The global achievement gap.* New York: Basic Books.

Zakaria, F. (2008). *The post-American world.* New York: Norton.

Zhao, Y. (2009). *Catching up or leading the way: American education in the age of globalization.* Alexandria, VA: ASCD.

# INDEX

The letter *f* following a page number denotes a figure.

# ABOUT THE AUTHOR

 Vivien Stewart is senior education advisor and former vice president at Asia Society, where she has been leading a national effort to prepare American students and educators for the interconnected world of the 21st century. She has worked with schools around the country to broaden students' educational experiences to prepare them for work and citizenship in a global age. She has worked with states to adapt their policies to a global knowledge economy, and she has developed resources for teachers to use to promote global knowledge and skills. Stewart has also used her unique international background in education to bring together education leaders from different countries to share expertise on how to respond to the rapid transformations of globalization and the need for world-class educational systems.

Prior to Asia Society, Stewart was director of education programs at Carnegie Corporation of New York, where she developed initiatives to improve early childhood and youth development and managed a series of influential national education task forces. She has also been a senior policy advisor at the United Nations and a visiting scholar at Teachers College, Columbia University, and she is an internationally known writer on education. She serves on the boards of a number of national education organizations.

Stewart received her undergraduate and graduate degrees from Oxford University and, in 2007, was awarded the Harold McGraw Prize for her contributions to international education. She can be reached at vstewart@asiasociety.org.

## Related ASCD Resources

At the time of publication, the following ASCD resources were available (ASCD stock numbers appear in parentheses). For up-to-date information about ASCD resources, go to www.ascd.org. You can search the complete archives of Educational Leadership at http://www.ascd.org/el.

### ASCD Edge

Exchange ideas and connect with other educators interested in global education, overseas/international schools, Common Core State Standards, and 21st century learning on the social networking site ASCD Edge™ at http://ascdedge.ascd.org/

### Print Products

*Breaking Free from Myths about Teaching and Learning: Innovation as an Engine for Student Success* (109041) by Allison Zmuda

*Catching Up or Leading the Way: American Education in the Age of Globalization* (#109076) by Yong Zhao

*Creating the Opportunity to Learn: Moving from Research to Practice to Close the Achievement Gap* (#107016) by A. Wade Boykin and Pedro Noguera

*Curriculum 21: Essential Education for a Changing World* by Heidi Hayes Jacobs (#109008)

*How to Teach Now: Five Keys to Personalized Learning in the Global Classroom* (#111011) by William Powell and Ochan Kusuma-Powell

*Understanding Common Core State Standards* (#112011) by John Kendall

*Wasting Minds: Why Our Education System Is Failing and What We Can Do About It* (#111015) by Ronald A. Wolk

### Videos

*21st Century Skills: Promoting Creativity and Innovation in the Classroom* (15-minute DVD and associated professional learning materials) (#609096)

*Assessment for 21st Century Learning* (3 DVD set) (#610010)

*The Signs and Sounds of Equitable Practices* (45-minute DVD) (#610013)

THE WHOLE CHILD The Whole Child Initiative helps schools and communities create learning environments that allow students to be healthy, safe, engaged, supported, and challenged. To learn more about other books and resources that relate to the whole child, visit www.wholechildeducation.org.

For more information: send e-mail to member@ascd.org; call 1-800-933-2723 or 703-578-9600, press 2; send a fax to 703-575-5400; or write to Information Services, ASCD, 1703 N. Beauregard St., Alexandria, VA 22311-1714 USA.